The Sandwich Years

The Sandwich Years

When Your Kids Need Friends and Your Parents Need Parenting

Dennis and Ruth Gibson

BAKER BOOK HOUSE
Grand Rapids, Michigan 49516

Copyright 1991 by
Baker Book House Company

ISBN: 0-8010-3839-1

Second printing, August 1991

Printed in the United States of America

Scripture quotations not otherwise identified are from the New International
Version, © 1973, 1978, 1984 International Bible Society. Used by permission
of Zondervan Bible Publishers.

Library of Congress Cataloging-in-Publication Data

Gibson, Dennis L.
   The sandwich years/Dennis and Ruth Gibson.
      p   cm.
   ISBN 0–8010–3839–1
   1. Middle age—United States. 2. Middle aged persons—United States—
Psychology. 3. Middle aged persons—United States—Life skills guides. I.
Gibson, Ruth. II. Title.
HQ1059.5.U5G53 1991
305.24′4′0973—dc20   90–46441
                                                        CIP

To

the Homebuilders I Sunday school class
at Wheaton Bible Church—

our peers
in the middle of the sandwich

Contents

Introduction

Dennis

"Grandma's really losing it, don't you agree, Marilyn?"
Jane was actually asking this question of her daughter
Kathy, but mistakenly called her "Marilyn," her own sister's name. Of course, Jane and Kathy later told Marilyn
about this slip of the tongue and they all laughed
about it.

A sense of humor helps us through many sticky problems. Jane and Marilyn, sisters in their fifties, have been
worrying about their eighty-two-year-old mother's grad-
ual loss of mental sharpness. Laughing at their own occasional blunders helps them handle anxiety and sadness
about their mother's increasing need for care and support.

Later that day Jane spent some earnest hours counseling her young adult daughter. Kathy needed some feedback from her mother to narrow the wide range of career
options open to her as a recent college graduate. It
occurred to Jane that she was called on to serve as parent
to two generations.

Sandwiched!

Like butter between two slices of bread, we in our thir-
ties through sixties find ourselves sandwiched between
our children and our parents. Although our adult children

need us less as parents and more as adult friends, our own parents are no longer able to care for themselves as they used to and increasingly need our help. Our nests have emptied, but we have new responsibilities toward the elderly members of our families.

(We have a friend in her eighties who found herself *still* sandwiched between two generations. Her mother was 101. Our friend moved into a retirement community and her mother moved to a nursing home. Until that time the daughter cared for the mother in her own home.)

Although many of us play tennis, ski, and ride bikes (but not as well as we did ten years ago)—and an envied few can still fit into athletic uniforms and cheerleading skirts from twenty-five years ago—we are in "the sandwich years." The signs are unmistakable. We notice that our doctors, dentists, lawyers, and ministers are the ages of our children. Some *are* our children. We make frequent visits to funeral homes to acknowledge the deaths of relatives, parents of our friends, and our older mentors. We suddenly notice that there have been several deaths in one month. As one acquaintance put it in a memorably humorous way during his sandwich years: "People are dying now who never used to die!" What an insight! Not just *persons* are dying before our eyes, but a whole generation that once seemed immortal, rock solid, always there for us.

We offer cross-generational comfort and receive it. As we help each other to grieve and flex and adjust, these wakes and funerals reverberate to us the bottom-line reality of our own mortality. The story comes down to us of a wise emperor of ancient Rome who delegated a servant to ride beside him during the triumphal processions. The servant was to notice when the cheers of the crowd rose to a crescendo and beguiled the emperor into vainglorious self-pride. At that strategic moment, the servant was to bend near the emperor's ear and whisper, "Remember, Caesar, you will one day die." The sandwich years' realities have a way of deflating our pretensions. As we suddenly become the *older* generation, we catch ourselves muttering, "It happened so fast!"

We are called on to sort through the belongings of a deceased loved one, feeling like voyeurs peeking at private things, as we go through files, letters, drawers, and closets. Somehow "things" lose their value, and we wonder if we will complete the garage sales of ancestors' belongings before someone has to sort through our own. We hate to think of our children having to deal with our personal files and collections—but they will. We start thinking like Mother Teresa, who supposedly once said, "If it takes you more than fifteen minutes to pack, you have too much stuff." (See chapter 16 on this subject.)

A Living Snapshot

Ruth and some friends she has known from gradeschool days got together recently in a nearby suburb when one of the gang flew in from out of town and created an occasion for a potluck supper. As Ruth entered the hostess's kitchen and put her pot of baked beans on the counter, she glanced through the glass patio door at the people assembled there and framed in the doorway. "They look so middle-aged!" Ruth remarked. Of course she felt immediately embarrassed at what she had blurted out in the shock of the moment. "They" were her kindergarten classmates—forty years later. You bet they looked middle-aged! Seeing some of them for the first time in many years, Ruth glimpsed a snapshot of life speeding by at breakneck pace.

As little kids we often asked peevishly, "Mommy, what can I do?" There were so many hours to fill. Summer days were long and luxurious in the 1940s before Milton Berle and Howdy Doody moved into our homes. Time stretched endlessly before us. Now we ask, "Where are the days going?" because we cannot find enough time to finish everything we would like to do.

We also notice that thirty-year-olds look "like teen-agers" to us. A young adult friend directs a summer camp. During a visit we made recently, he introduced his staff. "These fine staff members are college students and school-teachers," he said proudly. Not one of them looked a day past junior high, at least from our middle-aged vantage point.

Another friend, in his seventies and chairman of the board of a local college, recently addressed the incoming freshmen and their parents. He joked, "I used to think the freshmen looked so young. Now I think the fresh-men's *parents* look so young!"

Who We Are

At this writing, I am a fifty-two-year-old psychologist. My wife, Ruth (same age), works with me as a marriage-and-family counselor. Our three sons graduated from high school in the Midwest, went to college in California, grad-uated, and stayed on the West Coast. One of them recently married. We earn most of our livelihood by coun-seling individuals, couples, and families in our office in Wheaton, Illinois. We teach family-living seminars about marital communication and parent-child relations and also offer a seminar about "brief counseling" techniques, based on my earlier book, *Vitality Therapy* (Baker Book House, 1989). We co-host a weekly TV talk show called "Positive Living," which features these topics.

Both of my parents and Ruth's dad died in the past seven years. Ruth's happy, steady parents celebrated their golden wedding anniversary. My own volatile parents divorced when I was fourteen. They remarried each other twenty-five years later, soon fought again, separated, and lived out their own lives alienated from each other. We have seen many slices of life—through our own experi-ences and through the windows of the hundreds of fami-lies we have counseled.

Aims of This Book

It is our hope that this book will foster reconciliation between generations. Particularly, we want to help people in the sandwiched generation make sense of this period in their lives and thereby come to peace with their fallible loved ones. We will provide many illustrations to underscore some practical ideas toward reaching that goal. As each generation understands and respects the preceding one, we will all harvest the fruit of that commandment with a promise: "Honor your father and mother, that it may go well with you" (see Eph. 6:2–3).

Our hearts beat with the biblical promise surrounding a great prophet who was to come. His mission rings in the words that conclude the Old Testament: "He will turn the hearts of the fathers to their children, and the hearts of the children to their fathers" (Mal. 4:6).

Part One

Parents
to
Adult Children

1

Detaching

Dennis

Most of us in the sandwich years are past the days of cuddling our babies, bandaging grade schoolers' skinned knees, and dealing with our inscrutable teenagers. Now we face an even tougher job—affirming their independence as adults. Letting go—detaching—is what it's all about. We will always be their parents, but how we play that role must change, just as *they* have changed in what they need from us.

Diving into Life

In his mid-teens, our oldest son, Steve, read of a place in Ohio that trains people in sport-parachuting and sky-diving. He decided he wanted to go. I had never thought of such a thing but quickly supported the idea, seeing myself as the champion of Steve's emancipation. Ruth opposed the idea, viewing it as "insane to risk death by jumping from a plane." I sided with Steve and told Ruth we had to let go of the apron strings. Our little baby was growing up and we both needed to face the fact.

We spent some days debating and gathering information on parachuting and skydiving. Ruth called a nearby rural airport that offered such training and asked how safe it was. The person on the other end of the phone assured Ruth that it was very safe and popular and enjoyable. Ruth asked, "Well, have you had any fatalities?" The answer, after a pause, was: "Well, no *serious* fatalities." We decided *not* to train at that place!

Finally, as we talked out this issue, Ruth had a brainstorm. She said, "Okay, Dennis, I know that you have good judgment. I know you love Steve and do not want to see him hurt. So I want you to go along with Steve and evaluate the training. In fact, go through the training with him. Decide when Steve is completely prepared to jump safely. Then go up in the plane with him—and *you* jump first!"

I had never thought of *myself* parachuting. The idea jolted me, but I had to put my money where my mouth was. For the sake of my son's emancipation, I decided to go along with Ruth's suggestion.

When it came time for the training, Steve's younger brother David joined us. The whole family went to the training place in Ohio for the great event. We completed the preflight training in one day and looked forward to good weather for jumping on the morrow.

In the plane, I sat near the door, with Steve and Dave farther back, behind the jumpmaster. When we got to about five-thousand feet above the earth, the jumpmaster opened the door, which slammed against the side of the plane. My heart jumped up into my throat as I looked out onto Ohio cornfields below. *I'm going to die!* I thought, then muttered silently, "No way am I going to jump out of a perfectly good airplane."

I soon realized, however, that to chicken out now would require me to climb over my two sons and cower in the back of the plane. To endure their scornful looks of disrespect at that act of "cowardice" meant to me a fate even worse than death. I decided I *would* rather die than let my sons down!

I poised myself in the open door. At the jumpmaster's command I launched myself out into the wild blue yonder. The chute opened! Fear instantly gave way to pleasure. I enjoyed two or three of the most peaceful minutes of my life, floating under a beautiful open parachute. I would like to do it again someday.

David jumped from the plane twice that day, and Steve made five similar "static line jumps." This means that a cable hooked to the airplane pulls the parachute out of the pack strapped on the jumper's back as he plunges toward the earth. Going through the proper motions in five such jumps earned Steve the privilege of skydiving on his sixth. There would be no static line—he would have to pull his own ripcord—or die.

The rest of the family stood on the ground as the plane bearing Steve climbed higher and higher into the sky. Finally came the moment when a little black dot emerged from the plane and began falling through space. We were seeing Steve truly take his life in his own hands. No Mommy or Daddy could save him now. He had to use his own head and his own confidence, his own skill and good judgment, to keep himself alive. What relief we felt when we saw that beautiful colored mushroom puff open over his head!

That jump served as a kind of initiation into manhood for Steve. We, his parents, recognized it as such. Talk about letting go! Perhaps because we let Steve take his life in his own hands in such controlled adventures as this, he never wanted to do so in crazy ways, like taking drugs. Of course, we know that successful parenting is not all that simple! Timing, circumstances, and love and acceptance are all factors in the process. In our case, we are grateful that we did enough things correctly so that Steve was ready to leap into the adult world at the appropriate time.

Adult at Eighteen

Reader's Digest for May 1977 published an article titled, "Adult at Eighteen." The article tells specific ways that parents can gradually prepare their children to be financially responsible and self-reliant in every way. Ideally, parents will turn over more and more responsibilities to the children beginning in their early years. Then, by the time the children reach eighteen, they should be able to take responsibility for purchasing a car, financing their education, and paying for their own clothing and living expenses. A lofty goal? Not at all!

The article conveys the need for a sense of parental confidence in the children's capabilities. The author shows how to sidestep a jarring transition. When parents overprotect children for too long and then suddenly leave them on their own, the young people often stumble in early adulthood simply because they have not practiced adult skills early enough under the guidance of their parents.

As a case in point, years from now, historians may look back on ours as the last generation of middle-class families who could consider sending their kids to college. For many parents, college loan payments continue for years after the students have graduated. The article urges parents *not* to pay for college educations for their children! The author acknowledges that this idea sounds radical to people who ask, "Isn't this something we *owe* our children?" He goes on to argue: "If we have successfully made them into adults, they will find a way to get the education they need in a time and a place appropriate for them."

We know some parents who wish now that they had followed this advice when their children came to college age. Instead, they borrowed heavily to send them. They now find themselves paying off that debt while also providing for their own retirement. If you agree that seems like *too* much for one generation to do for another, consider these alternatives:

1. Students can choose a junior college near home instead of an expensive private college far away. If they have held part-time jobs during their high school days and while attending college, they can usually manage the fees on their own. Later, if they wish further higher education, they might transfer to a four-year college, also at their own expense.
2. I [Dennis] earned my way through engineering school on a cooperative work-study program. I went to school for a term, then worked for a term getting practical experience in industry.
3. In one family of eight children, the parents helped the first one pay for college. That one then helped the next younger and so on, until all made it through. The youngest eventually paid back Mom and Dad. What a marvelous alternative to sibling rivalry! (Whatever the actual source of a college loan, the *student*, not the parent, should be held accountable for repayment.)
4. Many colleges offer non-repayable financial-aid packages. Some of these grants go unclaimed because eligible students are unaware of their existence. Be sure to investigate every possible avenue of funding through the high school guidance office and the admissions office of the college in which the student is interested.

The Alaskan Pipeline

The Proposal

Each of our sons had a thirst for adventure. At around age sixteen, Steve announced that he planned to work on the Alaskan pipeline! At that time this massive engineering project had workers from the continental United States traveling to Alaska to build a crude-oil pipeline hundreds of miles across the wilderness. Steve dreamed of living out in the woods and earning tons of money on this rugged project. Although Ruth and I had graduated from college, we did not insist that our sons must attend college. We were willing to let them choose careers that did not require higher education. But in this instance, we felt Steve was testing us to see if we would allow him to make his own decision.

Steve announced to us that, *if* he finished high school, he certainly had no intention of going on to "something as dull as college." He explained that he would not need higher education, since that would merely prepare him for a "boring office job in a city." He would never agree to wear the uncomfortable shirt and tie that such work would require. Accordingly, he wanted to work on the Alaskan pipeline.

The "normal" parental response, on hearing thoughts like these from a teenager, is knee-jerk opposition: "What a crazy idea. I don't want to hear anymore talk of that kind." Such rigidity often pushes the kid into out-and-out rebellion. He or she may rush into fulfilling the dream, no matter how impractical it might be or how little planning is done.

To Steve's announcement, we answered, "Wow, that's exciting! If anybody can pull that off, you can. But tell us more about it."

Steve thereupon launched into explaining how he had heard that the construction project needed rugged young men by the hundreds, willing to brave the dangers and hardships of the Arctic. As he saw things, he could work most of the hours of most days earning "massive overtime" and piling up enough money "to live on Easy Street" when he came back home a year or two later.

Without attempting to dampen his enthusiasm, we eagerly asked, "Just how much *do* they pay?" At this realistic question our son balked a little bit and answered, "Well, I'm not exactly sure, but I know it's a lot." We went on with our plan to get him thinking:

"And where will you probably live? What will you eat?" Steve answered that he would probably rent or build a log cabin in the woods, buy a high-powered rifle, and live on moose meat.

We resisted the impulse to lecture our son about the Alaskan cold and that he would probably lose his fingers and toes to frostbite. As we continued to revel in his dream with him, we gently and subtly managed to help him see the possible drawbacks and impracticalities of his plan. By the time we asked him just *when* he thought he could leave on the project, he was a little vague, but said, "Maybe within a year or two."

Because we listened nonjudgmentally to his dream, our son did not *have* to go to Alaska to assert his independence. He finished high school, went to a college of his choice, and graduated. Today, he regularly wears a suit and tie in his challenging work in the corporate business world.

The Lesson

Often, when parents oppose their children's "impractical" schemes, the kids feel duty bound to go ahead, just to prove the parents wrong. Young people approaching adulthood sometimes focus so intently on the mission of showing that their parents cannot stop them that they lose sight of the potential dangers to themselves.

A wiser course than outright opposition and ridicule is for parents to draw upon the excitement their youngsters feel. Let them describe their wonderful dream in all its splendor. Then, especially as the kids advance beyond the idea stage and come to the brink of taking unwise action, you can guide them best by asking particular questions that will lead them to pause and think about *everything* involved.

You can be supportive without actually endorsing your kid's plan. For example, you might even say, "I may be wrong, but I have a hunch that this project may not turn out as promising as it seems. If I were in your shoes, I would not do it. However, I'm confident that, if you go ahead with it and it does not turn out well, you certainly have what it takes to make the best of the situation and turn it into a valuable learning experience." A vote of confidence often frees children from having to do foolish things to prove their individuality.

"You Two Weirdos"

I had just come in from jogging one evening and entered the kitchen where Ruth and Scott were just finishing up a conversation concerning Scott's disapproval of his mother's "cheerleading routines." Free-spirited Ruth often did cheers in our living room that she remembered from her high school days. She even teased Scott one time by saying she planned to lead a mothers' cheerleading squad at the half-time ceremonies of one of his high school football games. Scott felt great relief on learning that Ruth was joking, since he thought her cheerleading bordered on the weird.

Scott turned his attention next to what he considered another "weirdness" in his life, namely my tattered jogging clothes. I considered it thrifty to use old business clothes for jogging. Even if the knee was a little threadbare the pants would still do for running around the block. And if the weather was nippy, I wore an old suit jacket. Scott commented that people could easily mistake his father for a terrorist or a transient beggar. At any rate, our son did not want me running anywhere within sight of his school bus stop in the morning.

Scott, then the last remaining child at home, sat at the kitchen table eating a huge bowl of bedtime cereal. During this teasing conversation, we, his parents, stood with our arms around each other at the kitchen sink. Scott paused for a thoughtful moment, looked at us, and said affectionately, "Well, at least you two weirdos have each other."

What a profound statement! The youngest chick can

confidently leave the nest, knowing that Mom and Dad have each other. Many families have a tough time negotiating this significant transition. When moms and dads concentrate too much on their parental roles, they forget their relationship as husband and wife.

Many sensitive youngsters unconsciously recognize that their parents are not ready to be spouses with each other. Such kids may take the position of scapegoat and forgo their own emancipation efforts while they try to keep Mom and Dad from splitting up. They often resort to extreme misbehavior to give parents enough of a concern to keep them working together and avoiding the crisis of facing each other's own needs. (Ironically, if some of these manipulative tactics are partly for the sake of younger children in the home, an adolescent, too, may be "sandwiched.")

For Scott to call us "weirdos" conveyed an affectionate needling. It allowed him to distance himself from us while loving us. Because he knew we had each other, he was free to leave the nest in search of his own adult identity.

The PFD Rule

I once took our three grown children on a long-awaited father-son fishing trip to Canada. (I think I regarded the fishing more seriously than the boys did.) I made myself a stickler for safety and bought life jackets for all of us. Actually, they do not call these items "life jackets" anymore, but "personal flotation devices" (PFDs). The boys found these PFDs cumbersome and uncomfortable, but I insisted they wear them anyway.

Although I had looked forward to adult man-to-man comradeship with my grown sons on this trip, I now found myself in a position of being a dad having to discipline his sons to follow his rules. I could not escape the fact that we were in two generations. The boys loved to run the outboard motorboats in crazy circles for the sheer fun of it. Especially with that kind of zany activity going on, I in no way would consider backing down from the rule: each man had to wear a PFD whenever in a boat.

At one point my sons forced a showdown as we were about to head back to camp. The three together announced that they were taking off their PFDs. They said that nothing I could do would make them put them back on. They got quite a kick out of going on strike— three musketeers against their tyrant father.

Finally I had to pull my trump card. Only *I* knew the lake. Only *I* had a map. The boys could never find their way back to our campsite alone on this remote northern wilderness lake. So I went on a strike of my own: "I am not leaving this bay until your PFDs are on." To make my rule stick, I was willing to shiver through an entire night in the boat if necessary, just to outlast the boys in this contest of wills. They soon recognized this. They reluctantly put on their PFDs and kept them on.

That was a time when I felt lonely being "Dad." I envied the comradeship the boys had with each other. Although I wanted to break into that circle, I had to maintain the role of authority, which is different from that of "buddy." To put it another way, I felt painfully the fact that I was the unadorned filling between the two slices of bread that put me in the sandwich years. There in the wilderness, far from my bride, I felt the loneliness of being temporarily a "single parent" excluded from the generation of my children.

A Job at Disney World

One glorious year, all three of our sons attended the same college in California, but during their Christmas break our whole family traveled to Florida, where Ruth's mother and father had a place. While there, we enjoyed a couple of days at Walt Disney World. Our youngest son, Scott, discovered that the Disney organization was taking applications for college students to work summer jobs there. The idea appealed to him, so he thought he might pick up an application form.

The idea of Scott's working at Disney World was massively appealing to Ruth, too. She got so worked up that she began exclaiming, "Oh, yes, let's go right over to the administration office and get the sign-up form. Is there time? I'll help you fill it in, Scott."

At this strategic point, our oldest son, Steve, wisely took his mother aside. He said, "Mom, if you keep being this excited, you are going to kill this whole idea for Scott."

Suddenly, Ruth realized the truth of Steve's warning. Parents can get so enthusiastic about a young person's idea that they take it over and make it their own. The kid is then thrown back into feeling like a toddler again—complying with parental wishes—instead of an individual entitled to his or her own interests, plans, and dreams.

As it turned out, Scott never did pick up that application form. He set his sights on another summer adventure instead. And we never really knew for sure whether his mother's overenthusiasm for the Disney World idea had anything to do with his changing his mind.

An Afterword

Be ready to support your children's independence as they plan their higher education and careers, even if their choices are different from what you had hoped. If they earn an honest living, be grateful. Some kids are made to feel like failures because they don't live up to parental expectations for "prosperity" or "prestige." Do not insist that they adhere to *your* definitions of success and happiness or pressure them to chase after your own unfulfilled dreams.

Of course, even after our children have detached physically from our presence, they will need to know that we continue to affirm them as unique individuals. Appreciate today's accomplishments and yesterday's best efforts. Ruth remembered to do just that one day after David—

our "handyman" son—had left home. As she wandered through the house, she happened to notice all the improvements David had made through the years. There was the hole he had fixed in a wall, the laundry tub he had propped up, the room he had paneled, and the large address numerals he had installed at the front of the house. Ruth sat down to make a list of them all and sent it off to David as part of a thank you note for being our son.

2

Enjoying Each Other
Ruth

Have your fledglings already taken flight to establish a new nesting place and fulfill their destinies without your direct support? You will miss them, of course, especially the sounds of childish delight as they discovered what you had to show them about the world. But the days of family fun need not be over. You can enjoy each other's company *now*. If you can be "good friends" as well as "parent and child," those precious family ties will remain unbroken over the years, even if temporarily weakened by multi-generational differences of opinion.

Thirty Questions

A few years after graduating from college, our oldest son, Steve, took a new job in San Francisco. Several months later, I was invited to visit him there for a mother-son weekend to savor his new life. Steve excitedly welcomed me. He graciously hosted me in his apartment and proudly toured me around his newly adopted city.

I made the most of these unique few days with my

firstborn by taking the occasion to play with Steve a subtle variation of the game "Twenty Questions." At different times during our weekend, I asked Steve some questions from a list totaling thirty that I had prepared ahead
of time. These aimed at helping me understand Steve's
current adult identity. Even more, they put a capstone on
Steve's childhood for both of us by reviewing what it had
meant to him. We enjoyed the conversations aroused by
the questions, which are reproduced below:

 1. How do you think your birth order affected your expe-
    riences and our parenting of you?
 2. How many children do you want to have and why?
 3. How do you think you would be different if you had a
    sister?
 4. What is your perspective on Mom's having worked out-
    side the home?
 5. What is your perspective on Dad's years in graduate
    school? His switching jobs? Our moving several times?
 6. What do you consider the best place we ever lived?
 7. Where do you consider the best place possible to live?
 8. What do you consider the best school you attended?
 9. Who was the best teacher you ever had? Why?
10. What did Cub Scouts mean to you? Little League?
11. How could we have done better with your Christian
    education?
12. Who was your best Sunday school teacher? What made
    that teacher good for *you?*
13. How could people have made Sunday school better for
    you?
14. How could Mom and Dad have done better over the
    years in reaching our neighbors for Christ?
15. What perspective do you now have on jobs you had in
    high school? At the drugstore? The car wash? The long
    hours of cemetery lawn mowing?

16. How did your youth-group involvement affect you?

17. Who are your best friends?

18. How would you summarize the impact on you of the years you spent in each of the places you lived since college?

19. What did playing the cello in fourth grade mean to you? Why did you stop when you did? Have you ever wished you had continued? Or taken up some other instrument?

20. What do you remember from the bowling team you were on as a kid the year we lived in Nebraska?

21. What have you learned from us about marriage?

22. Who has influenced you most besides our family? How?

23. How can families, schools, and churches do a better job of preparing kids for marriage? For adult life in general?

24. How do you think that TV, movies, and popular music have affected your growing up?

25. How does the unique San Francisco lifestyle impinge on your own life?

26. What kinds of pressures do you get from single women?

27. What qualities do you most value in a potential life partner?

28. What are your standards on drugs and alcohol? How did you come to those?

29. When you come to the end of your life and look back over it, what do you most want to be able to say?

30. If earning a living were no consideration, how would you choose to spend the rest of your life?

No, I did not sit down with Steve and fire these questions at him as if it was an interrogation session! Rather, these were all topics we managed to touch on in an informal manner during our visit together. We learned a lot about each other in the process.

I learned much about my son that day, things I had never really thought deeply about before. In turn, I believe that Steve—because he realized that his ideas mattered to me—learned more about me, not just as "Mom," but as a caring adult who respected his views, even those that might not quite agree with my own.

"Thirty Questions" may not be the type of game you can comfortably play with your own children (whatever their ages), but perhaps you get the idea. In varying degrees, they cover a lot of ground in pointing representatives of two generations toward mutual respect and enjoyment of each other's company.

A Memento

During that visit I paid to Steve's apartment in San Francisco, I noticed a framed cut-out on his bookshelf. This decorative item stood out in the sleek, spare style that Steve, the orderly twenty-eight-year-old bachelor, seemed otherwise to prefer.

Inside the frame appeared the words "O Happy Day" on a plain black background. I puzzled over the meaning of this item, since so few artifacts graced Steve's neat, tasteful space. Then Steve told me the story behind "O Happy Day."

It seemed that while Grandma Gibson lived at "605," the unfinished attic of the two-bedroom brick bungalow formed a wonderland of fascination for our three young boys. Uncle Norman had used this attic as his private living space during his college years. He had tacked posters and pictures to the walls and ceiling around his bed, changing them from time to time.

We visited "605" one holiday season when our boys were grade school age. As usual, they crept into the attic for some new adventure. While they played and giggled there, Uncle Norman came upstairs. He slowly and deliberately added another item to his wall collection. The new item consisted of the cheery words "O Happy Day" in large type, torn from a magazine. The three young boys intently watched Uncle Norman at work.

On all subsequent visits, the boys raced up to the attic to see what had changed. Each time they confirmed that "O Happy Day" still occupied the place that Uncle Norman had assigned it. For years, that single item stood as a symbol of something stable in our boys' lives. Although they lived in five different homes during grade school, Grandma's attic stayed the same.

When Grandma finally sold "605," Scott helped her move. While cleaning out the attic, he noticed "O Happy Day" and carefully removed it from the wall it had graced for about fifteen years. He framed it tastefully to give as a housewarming present for his brother Steve's move to new quarters.

When Steve received the gift, he needed no words of explanation. "O Happy Day" summarized a chunk of childhood he and his brothers had shared.

I took it as an honor when Steve let me in on this story. When I joined my sons as keepers of a treasure— "O Happy Day"—I learned the following lessons:

Life consists of tiny points of experience that form stories. Like verbs and nouns in a library, they hold meaning only because of how someone hung them together. Little things have big meanings. We do well to frame them— either literally, or by prayer, tears, stories, litanies of remembrance. Such mementos matter a lot, especially when shared with loved ones.

Traditions and Rituals

Our family had just finished an enjoyable few days visiting first Disney World and then Epcot Center in Florida. In sight of the large aluminum dome, we gathered in a circle and repeated a ritual that stretched twenty years back into our lives with each other as a family. We commented on how good the time had been. We recalled many memorable events, offering each remark as an informal conversational prayer.

When we had finished our shared remembering, we

recited John 3:16, as the boys and I had done day after day as I saw them off to grade school. Then we sang our version of an old song that I had heard Boy Scouts sing in solemn day-ending ceremonies when I was a girl:

> Day is done.
> Gone the sun,
> from the land,
> from the hills,
> from the sky.
> All is well.
> Safely rest.
> God is nigh—'Night, Scouts.

At the end of our "ceremony," we paused, looked at each other, and at a nod from Dad, pronounced in unison, "Boop!" We borrowed that sound from computer technology. After you type something onto the screen of a personal computer, you review it to see if you have it just the way you want it. Then you hit the "Enter" key, and the machine makes a sound like "Boop." Our family employs the term as a sort of high-tech "Amen." We speak of booping activities as a way of indicating that we have completed, approved, and digested them.

Incidentally, when I did my "Thirty Questions" review with Steve, he mentioned that daily repetition of John 3:16 at the doorway. He said that it stood in his mind as a reliable truth about life, associated with the reliability of the loving Mom who made it happen every day. God assures us in Scripture: " . . . my word that goes out from my mouth . . . will not return to me empty, but will accomplish what I desire and achieve the purpose for which I sent it" (Isa. 55:11).

We continue another tradition each Christmas Eve. As an eight-year-old girl I acquired a pen pal overseas. Ever since I have continued my correspondence with Miss Audrey E. Pierson of Whitley Bay, Northumberland, England. I even visited Audrey's home once during the year I worked as an airline flight attendant before I married Dennis. I discovered that the Pierson family always remembered me and other dear friends in an eggnog toast on Christmas Eve. We adopted this tender tradition into our own family, calling it our toast to my "pen pal in England." Our boys mistakenly heard it as "Pen Pal O'Winga," and thus renamed Audrey. Some families close in too much on themselves, as in the motto "It's us against the world." Our yearly inclusion of Pen Pal O'Winga in our family's love has helped us to stretch just a little to a global perspective: "It's us *and* our world."

Whenever we are together as a family, Dennis frequently reaches forth his large right hand toward each one of our boys and intones, "I give you my paternal hand of blessing." He takes the position of patriarch, in the tradition of Abraham, Isaac, and Jacob. One time, during a Thanksgiving gathering of the Gibson family in Kansas City, our youngest son could not join us. Scott phoned on Thanksgiving Day and received in the course of his call a paternal blessing from Dennis that went something like this:

> As the sun beams brightly from the clear blue sky, I call forth upon you the radiance of God's great fatherly love. May it soak deep into your innermost being, nourish your soul, and grow within you the acorn seeds of wisdom into oaks of righteousness in your character. May it bring deep satisfaction to you and bountiful enrichment to the lives of those to whom you extend a hand of blessing by your lively smile and warm words of affirmation.

Dennis told me afterward that Scott had paused for a reverent moment after this heartfelt blessing. Then he had quipped, "Dad, the phone is glowing!"

A Phoned "I Love You"

Since they left home, we have enjoyed our sons by long-distance phone calls once or twice a week. At one point we noticed that they began regularly ending each call by saying, "I love you." During their teen years they would not have considered making such a tender statement.

We wondered what had happened. Were they following the example we had set in saying, "I love you," to them or to *our* parents? Maybe some older person told them something like: "You know, you will not always have your parents around. Appreciate them while you can."

We still have not gotten a straight answer from our boys concerning how they decided to start this precious practice. At any rate, it makes us proud of their manliness in being willing to do it. And it serves for them the valuable purpose of detaching from us. How can such a loving action foster *de*-taching? Because they *choose* to do it without our prompting. We did not require it of them. Kids emancipate more fully by designing their own ways to cherish their parents than by rebelling against them.

About Grandchildren

When our friends in the sandwich years become grandparents, they tell us they get all the joys of having children without the headaches. This time around with infants, they say, they know what to expect better than they did as first-timers. Here follow some of their ideas on how to love your grandchildren while respecting your children as *their* parents.

Merging Traffic. Geographical distance may keep you from seeing grandchildren often. When you do visit, get acquainted (or re-acquainted) in a slow, relaxed manner. Don't overwhelm the little ones by coming on strong to make up for lost time. In between visits, keep in touch with notes and cards, preferably with some snapshots of Grandma and Grandpa.

A child can behave well for an hour, but in a week-long visit, the child's imperfections will show. Use these problem times to show "love, joy, peace, patience, kindness, goodness, faithfulness, gentleness, and self-control . . ." (Gal. 5:22–23).

We often counsel adults who can define one of these fruits of the Spirit by telling of a grandparent who was a living example of it. Our own adult children also continue to learn by watching how *we* handle stresses that deluge us.

Material Things. Be wary of giving too many material gifts. (Especially do not create an arena of competition with the other grandparents.) Specialize in giving gifts of time and self: a walk, playing in the snow, making cookies, going fishing, reading a book, telling stories, talking together to Jesus.

We fondly remember Grandpa Flesvig's joy when he would take eighteen-month-old Steve in his arms and walk out to a small woods near our house. There the two of them shook snow off low branches of the trees—to their mutual delight.

Plant Memories. Grandma and Grandpa once took six-year-old Steve to the top of the Foshay Tower in Minneapolis, where we lived during Dennis's years in graduate school. Steve still speaks of the feeling of security he had as Grandpa's arms held him firmly atop what then stood tallest of all buildings in the Twin Cities. Years later, as a computer salesman, Steve returned to the Foshay Tower while on business in Minneapolis. He reported to Grandma about that visit. He told her that—although nearby buildings now dwarf the tower—he recalled the tower of strength he saw in his trustworthy Grandpa, now physically gone from his life but alive in Steve's memory bank.

Who's in Charge? Bolster your children's position as managers of their households. Recognize that they have to work hard to learn a lot of parenting skills that took *you* years of stumbling to acquire. They, too, will make mistakes and may ask for your feedback. (Be wary of volunteering "advice"!) After a crisis in their household cools—and they want to discuss it with you—engage them in conversations that encourage them. Start off by citing the positive things you were aware that they did. Give three compliments for each negative comment, and no more than one negative per conversation. Intervene more strongly *only* if you see physical or emotional abuse. Even then, be aware that your perception may be faulty.

Give Their Parents a Break. Offer to sit with your grandchildren so that their dad and mom can spend time together as husband and wife. It will be a pleasant interlude for you, and it provides for them a change of pace that can reap dividends for the entire family way out of proportion to what it costs you in time.

An Afterword

It is never too late to speak of love. Few relationships have not had their solidarity threatened at one time or another by past misunderstandings that continue to undermine their mutual enjoyment of the present. If there are any alienated feelings in your own family, you—the parent—can take the first step toward repairing the damage. One way to start is to let your child know about the things you miss, now that he or she has left home. Even the strongest family needs occasional reminders of what has bound them together.

Reminding a child of a pleasure you once shared expresses your love in a tangible way, which may be all it takes to reopen a door of understanding. For example, one mother stood in her living room one day and was suddenly struck by its silence as she remembered her daughter's piano playing, which once filled the home with delightful sounds. Although the two had quarreled recently and been out of touch for weeks, Mom picked up the phone to thank her daughter for that pleasant memory. Those simple words of appreciation struck a responsive chord because they underscored enjoyable moments they had once shared.

So, too, can we all enrich our present years and brighten the outlook for the future. Our adult children's world may be quite different from our own, but we need not exist on separate planes of time and space.

3

Your Last Chance to Discipline

Dennis and Ruth

A major part of parental responsibility is disciplining our children for their own benefit. When they were very young, the "Just do it" approach usually sufficed. Although adolescents need rules, too, the emphasis must now shift from making simple directives to applying more subtle pressure. Now is that last chance to discipline. But if our young adults do not understand and accept the reasoning behind our standards, they will usually rebel as a show of independence.

The Driver's License

When Archie, the son of friends of ours, approached the magic age of sixteen, he could hardly wait to get his driver's license. His parents, who realized that he was going through a phase of disrespect toward authority, wisely welcomed the leverage that the driver's license gave them. Archie needed their signature to take the examination for his license, but he seemed to consider it a right rather than a privilege. He rather disdainfully told his parents that they *had* to sign the form.

Archie could hardly believe it when they informed him that they wanted to "think about it for a while." He continued to put pressure on them. This convinced them more than ever that they needed to make their signature contingent on some ongoing demonstration from him that he knew how to respect authority and recognized the responsibilities that went with a driver's license.

The Principle

By the time a child reaches the middle teenage years, parents have lost much of the leverage they formerly relied upon to coerce the child into obedience. When parents no longer have greater physical size or strength than the child, threats of punishment, such as spankings or "go to your room," fall on deaf ears. One of the few tangible pieces of leverage remaining is parental consent for a driver's license or teenage work permit. Archie's parents decided to make maximum use of this advantage to achieve a significant step of growing up for their son.

After some days of thinking, they came up with a program by which Archie could earn their signature. They wanted him to learn several things in the process:

1. To restrain his impulse to speak to them in a disrespectful tone of voice.
2. To apologize when he had slipped into a scornful tone of voice and to recover into a more adult attitude.
3. To read some books that would give him an underpinning in Christian character.
4. To be motivated to finish work he had begun on an old Jeep. (This project had become so discouraging that he rarely touched it any more. And it was taking up the whole garage!)

The System

Mom and Dad worked out a point system by which Archie could earn Dad's signature for his driver's exam. They put it in writing as follows:

Requirements
Pass driver-education course.
Pay car-insurance premium of $150 from your savings.
Accumulate 1,000 points by methods described below.

Point system

(Dad would keep track of all gains and losses and totals at end of each day.)

Read and report on books from the list below. Report orally to Mom and Dad, emphasizing what you got out of the book personally. (*Add* 200 points per book.)

Stop nagging and pestering and say "Okay" when told "No" is our final answer to any request you make. (*Add* 20 points. Maximum of one per day.)

Continued pestering after being told to stop. (*Subtract* 20 points per incident.)

Ask Dad before wearing any of his clothing. (*Add* 10 points. Maximum of one per day.)

Wearing something of Dad's without asking. (*Subtract* 10 points per item.)

Complete a wilderness learning program such as Outward Bound. (*Add* 200 points.)

Pay $20 toward cost of above program. (*Add* 10 points.)

Use of abusive language. (*Subtract* 10 points per time.)

Continued use of abusive language, or rough treatment of siblings, or throwing a tantrum after being told to stop. (*Subtract* 50 points per incident.)

Demonstrate an attitude of respect toward Mom and Dad when they announce a rule in any area of your life, by (1) showing that you understand. (Say our rule and our reasons back to us in your own words, until we agree that what you are saying is the same as what we mean.) And (2) telling us in calm, matter-of-fact wording any objections you have to our rule, and what you propose instead. (*Add* 50 points for each instance.)

Demonstrate an attitude of cooperativeness by cheerfully agreeing to do some job requested by Mom or Dad, even if you dislike the inconvenience. (*Add* 20 points for each instance.)

Griping, whining, or disrespectful protest to above type of request. (*Subtract* 10 points per request.)

Remove Jeep parts and bike parts from outside house, leaving room for us to park one car and space to walk around it in the garage. (*Add* 100 points, but if Jeep and bike parts are still outside on July 18, Mom and Dad will dispose of them while you are away on a trip.)

Make progress on fixing Jeep as follows:

Engine clean and put together	(50 points)
Fuel system functional	(50 points)
Cooling system in and filled	(50 points)
Electrical system functional	(50 points)
Brakes functional	(50 points)
Exhaust, steering, and transmission systems functional	(50 points)
Repair flooring	(50 points)
Drive once around block with Dad	(100 points)

Book List

Basic Christianity, John R. W. Stott
Man's Search for Meaning, Viktor Frankl
Mere Christianity, C. S. Lewis
The Screwtape Letters, C. S. Lewis
Your God Is Too Small, J. B. Phillips

The Results

Archie received this written point program with mild protest. He did not like the idea that he would have to *do* something to earn the driver's license he so urgently wanted. However, he seemed to feel a little bit calmed by the very fact that his parents had responded in a firm and specific manner. They showed respect for him by avoiding the generalizations and accusations that rebellious teenagers often provoke on the part of their elders.

Parents often swing from one extreme to another and thereby send mixed messages to their teenagers. Sometimes parents feel like giving up and decide that they don't want to fight over the issue. Then they say things like, "I can't control you anymore. You have a mind of your own."

Other times they swing to the opposite extreme and overdo their attempts at control by removing *all* privileges.

They might say on an angry impulse, "You're grounded for the rest of the year!" They lose the youngster's respect if they enact unrealistic standards or punishment and back down later.

Archie saw that his parents meant business and would hold firm regardless of his initial tantrums over their program. When he said, "This is stupid," they answered that it was the best plan they could think of at the time. They told him they would welcome any specific modifications he might recommend since they wanted it to seem both fair to him and beneficial in their eyes. Since he had only an objection to the idea in general, he finally uttered a few more grumbles and started in working the plan.

Archie's attitude did improve remarkably in the next few weeks. Mom and Dad looked back upon it as a significant turning point in his maturity. The state was asking them for their signature as a way to let their fellow citizens know how mature they considered their son. Did he show the judgment and respect for the law that would equip him to be a trustworthy driver on the roads of our land? They told their son that they could not attest to his respect of the state's authority until he convinced them that he would respect *their* authority.

Interestingly enough, about five years later this son found himself in a position of leadership over rebellious young teenagers. He challenged them to read a couple of those books that his parents had listed for him.

Planned Adventures in Living

We have seen several young persons during their late adolescent years make tremendous strides in growing up in a matter of weeks. Such dramatic turnarounds can sometimes come about through unusual experiences away from home. Difficult "wilderness programs," such as those sponsored by Outward Bound, often serve this purpose beautifully. As the young persons get away from home and their usual escapes, comforts, and conveniences, they cannot rely on the excuses they often use to sidestep their own responsibility. Neither can they hide behind the hovering presence of Mom and Dad nor evade being held accountable by focusing on flaws in others, including their parents.

Since, in the wilderness, the available resources are sparse and unfamiliar, the kids have to reach within themselves to develop their own solutions and coping techniques. They also have to learn to cooperate with the other people in their group who depend on them and on whom they depend for survival itself. Like it or not, they must conform to some basic rules. They simply will not get back to civilization if they do not follow the specified program. This gives the participants a dramatic experience of self-discipline—having to relate to certain rules, yet exercising their own competence within that framework.

These kids go through a series of labor pains in some very agonizing situations. Something new comes to life within them in the process. We might call it dignity, or self-esteem, or confidence. Parents can see it in the attitude and bearing of these young people when they come back home. They seem to stand taller. They look adults in the eye and talk directly with them more effectively than they did a few months before. They have grown in stature in every dimension. Without the opportunity to be challenged *away from home*, most kids typically develop this kind of maturity more slowly, often over a period of years.

Besides wilderness adventures, certain mission projects involve rigorous hard work and disciplined study. These well-planned programs put kids into stressful situations with leaders available to help them make it through. These trained adults help the young people connect their fresh experiences with timeless spiritual disciplines. Organizations such as Teen Missions often take middle-class youngsters overseas for such projects. Comfortable North American teenagers gain a valuable perspective through seeing poverty up close. It gives them a sense of appreciation for benefits (and parents) they have taken for granted.

We think so highly of away-from-home experiences that we have set a policy for ourselves. Every time we hear that young acquaintances are raising financial support for such a project, we donate some money. We ask the persons afterward specifically how they benefited from the experience, helping them crystalize for themselves what it meant to them.

Some people say they think all young people should have a period in military service before going on to college. They recommend it as "seasoning" to help them learn discipline and to take care of themselves while serving their country. Instead, we favor wilderness and mission experiences that give some structure to the kids' *moral* development as well. Military life often exposes kids to massive temptations without providing values and support for making morally based decisions. Without some ethical guidelines, they may develop bad habits that outweigh the excellent lessons they learn in the narrow areas of discipline, decision making, and physical skills.

Our sons had the good fortune to have some young adults come into their lives at a strategic time: when they were making the transition to their own budding adult identities. At least two youth leaders influenced our sons in the same direction that we had always considered the right one. Thus our sons had the chance to embrace the example of these other adults and consider it their own, rather than thinking of themselves as capitulating to parental pressures. A youth leader at a church—or in a Christian organization like Young Life, Youth for Christ, Fellowship of Christian Athletes, or another similar organization—can act as an outside reinforcement of the best influences within the home. Such contacts also serve as excellent training for leadership. We have seen our sons learn skills as high schoolers that served them well in corporate life as adults.

The Slothful "Loser"

Roots of the Problem

We often counsel families in which the parents have a hard time *letting* their kids fail! Parents naturally feel the urge to step in and overprotect children who have physical illnesses or allergies or other handicaps, but some parents cannot bear even to see their kids get a low grade on a school project—so they do the work *for* them.

Understandable? Perhaps. The motivation may be as straightforward as not wanting a child to feel "inferior." Or it may be more self-serving, as in "What will the neighbors think if Johnny is left back?" But children have to fail (fall short of the mark) sometimes. Otherwise—if we make things too easy for them—they will learn to look for parental bailouts or will set for themselves only "easy" goals that are unworthy of their abilities.

We know of one mother who stayed up all night rewriting a term paper that her son had completed that day to *his* satisfaction. "Just plain lazy" was Mom's assessment, but the son complained to us that he felt he was attending high school for Mom's sake, not his own. (He remembered in his preschool years that Mom would not allow him to color with crayons in a new coloring book until he could keep inside the lines.) "Fear of failure," in this case, should have been properly channeled so that the lad (1) was not made to adhere to Mom's questionable and too-rigid standards, and (2) was motivated to succeed in a course of study *he* chose. No wonder he seemed "just plain lazy"!

The Effects

When parents always pick up the pieces for their children, they tend to create one of two types of crises later. Some kids rebel in their teen years and tell their parents off, either loudly and plainly, or with passive-aggressive defiance, like failing in school. These are usually the ones that desperate parents bring to counselors during high school years.

More compliant youngsters let the parents keep doing things for them. As they become overly dependent on the parents, they have little inclination or courage to face the rigors of ordinary adult life. Their parents come to us later—exasperated with "children" in their mid-twenties who lie around the house not caring for themselves, not finding or keeping jobs, coming in at any hour of day or night, barking out orders to Mom and Dad, and complaining about their own "bad luck." These parents have unwittingly reared spoiled tyrants who have been conditioned to take for granted everything that has been done for them.

Because such parents have not detached from their child over a period of time, they now face the wrenching task of doing it all at once with an uncooperative adult. Their dilemma resembles that of families with an addicted member. In this case, the slothful son or daughter is as hooked on parental indulgences as an alcoholic is to the bottle.

These parents share a complementary addiction as codependents. They enable or encourage the child's addiction by indulging their own compulsion to be "perfect parents" whose children never fail or suffer. Ironically, they may justify their actions as "love." We do not often see such unhealthy relationships change until there is some kind of external crisis: the child gets put in jail, or a parent's health fails.

Disciplining a Young Adult

Perhaps you have been a basically good parent who has done most of the right things to detach from your child yet have still ended up with a twenty-four-year-old helpless baby in the house. When you finally decide to wean the youth—and you *must*—we recommend that you not just announce, "That's it, you're out of this house today!" Instead, offer him or her a reasonable number of opportunities to choose between responsible action and loss of a privilege that you have been providing.

For example, "From this point on I will no longer be doing your laundry. I am willing to show you how to run the washer and dryer. But if you want clean clothes, it's up to you to arrange it." You cannot force a young adult to do laundry; you can simply say that *you* will not do it.

Then, if the young adult still never does any laundry but wears stinky, filthy clothing, you can deliver an ultimatum: "Beginning at 12:01 P.M. tomorrow, you are welcome in this house only when wearing clothing that I find acceptable. Furthermore, I will no longer tolerate your storage in this house of any clothing items that I find objectionable. If you have not by then begun a laundering program that meets my standards, you must move out of the house." When the precise deadline arrives without your conditions being met to your satisfaction, your child has only two choices: move out or be evicted by the police. And you must be ready to make good on your threat without allowing for "one more chance"!

For wisdom in handling the most difficult situations, we recommend a book by a husband-and-wife team who adopted and raised several troublesome teenagers. The book is *How to Deal with Your Acting-Up Teenager*, by R. T. Bayard and J. Bayard (New York: M. Evans & Co., 1983). For general principles on how to exercise parental firmness with less serious issues, we suggest *Family Rules*, by Dr. Kenneth Kaye (New York: Walker & Co., 1984).

An Afterword

How can you maintain your firmness in not doing for young adults what they can and should do for themselves? You must decide that you are willing for them to be homeless and destitute if they don't tend to their own needs! That is what some call "tough love."

Take a moment to consider what might happen to your adult children if you were to die tomorrow. Would they be able to make it on their own? If you think not, you need to start enforcing some drastic measures today—as you begin their long-overdue training in survival.

4

Preparing Them for Marriage
Dennis and Ruth

Years ago, a Presbyterian minister named Charlie Shedd helped his daughter, Karen, prepare for her upcoming marriage in a loving and appropriate way. For months he wrote her letters touching on points of wisdom for her coming role as wife. When Karen was a married woman, she found that Dad's letters had helped her so much that she wanted others to benefit from them. She suggested that Dad publish them in book form. We often give Charlie Shedd's book as a wedding or shower gift: *Letters to Karen* (Nashville, Tenn.: Abingdon Press, 1965). Charlie later wrote his son, Philip, a corresponding series of letters that outlined a husband's role. We also recommend that book: *Letters to Philip* (Old Tappan, N. J.: Revell, 1968).

Obviously, Charlie Shedd did not wait until his children were engaged before he began to cultivate the kind of relationship with them that would later make his "premarital counseling" so meaningful. And neither can *we* shirk the responsibility to teach our children the principles of sexual morality and marital commitment that prepare them for the day they will be "forsaking all others" for a lifetime partner.

"Parental Guidance" and Movies

As our sons were growing up, we took seriously the "PG" concept of rating movies. Whether in a theater or on the TV in our home, we made a point of watching the movies that they watched and critiquing them afterward.

Suppose a movie portrayed sex between unmarried partners as if it were "no big deal." We might later lead a discussion with our boys (and any other guests who watched it) that would raise questions such as these:

How did the characters in this movie justify breaking God's law against fornication?

What flaw do you see in their reasoning?

How could you answer their thinking in a way consistent with biblical morality?

Why do you think *we* oppose this ungodly behavior?

We pointed out how one movie after another casually depicted sex outside marriage as normal, healthy, and commonplace. To us, the fact that these movies included such messages, even when they were not essential to the plot, was seductive propaganda. Since, obviously, movie producers did not get together and spontaneously decide on a policy to promote immorality, we wondered what influence could so coordinate their plans. So we taught about Satan's activity as the adversary of God's kingdom. We referred to Scriptures that our discussion brought to life, such as Ephesians 6:12—that we are in a spiritual warfare, that our enemies represent evil, and that we are to fight energetically in God's army.

Although we tried to make our movie discussions interesting, one of our sons would occasionally say in a disgruntled tone of voice, "Do we *have* to talk about it? Can't we just see the movie and chalk it off as being entertainment rather than moral instruction?" Our answer was that we *did* have to talk about the movie together before they could have our consent to watch another one.

We believe that sessions of this kind can serve to inoculate young people against evil influences. Medical science has virtually eradicated smallpox by vaccinations that result in a small, manageable case of the disease. An inoculated person's bloodstream builds up antibodies that will later fight off a potentially deadly invasion of the disease organisms. Similarly, kids who have seen and heard arguments for immorality, and learned to dispute them, have more resistance to temptation than if they had been completely insulated from its dangers.

Teaching from Scripture

The writer of Proverbs earnestly sought to prepare his son for a godly approach to human relationships. The entire fifth and seventh chapters dwell on the topic of sexual morality. These lessons should be incorporated into the regular spiritual feeding times that you provide for your children, especially as they enter adolescence.

Include also the plain teaching of Scripture about homosexuality, incest, and fornication. A summary of these commands appears in Leviticus 18 and 20, but there are many other Scripture references to proper use of our God-given sexuality. Use a commentary that helps to clarify any unclear ancient customs and a concordance to locate specific teachings. Don't let the kids dismiss the commands as "outdated." Relate biblical teachings to modern impurities, such as pornographic magazines set forth on the local drugstore newsstand.

Do not hesitate to show that God is so serious about

these laws that he specifies the death penalty for certain violations! Let us inform the younger generation of the biblical standards that are unchanging, though some people in our day reject them. Some self-appointed authorities, for example, refer to homosexuality as "an alternative and acceptable sexual preference." God plainly calls it an abomination worthy of capital punishment (Lev. 20:13).

The following Scriptures serve well as general guidelines in *every* area of life and should be reviewed with your children as you prepare them for marriage:

> But seek first his kingdom and his righteousness, and all these things will be given to you as well (Matt. 6:33).

> Do not be yoked together with unbelievers. For what do righteousness and wickedness have in common? . . . What does a believer have in common with an unbeliever? (2 Cor. 6:14–15).

Two Rooms!

We know a wise single mother who found a way to influence her adult son toward moral purity. Fred lived far from home and spent a lot of time with his girl friend, Linda. Two of Linda's relatives had to cancel plans for a trip to the Caribbean. Since they could not get refunds for their airline tickets, they gave them to Linda, who invited Fred to take the trip with her. Being thrifty young adults, they decided to save money on the hotel bill by sharing an inexpensive room with one bed.

When they told Fred's mom, she opposed the idea of this unmarried couple sharing the same room. As Christians, Fred and Linda both held premarital chastity as an important value. But they felt sure they could sleep in the same bed and not have sex. When Mom expressed doubt, Fred answered peevishly, "What's the matter, Mom, don't you trust me?" After that conversation,

Mom responded with a letter to her son, portions of which are reprinted below:

> We talked last night about your plans to share a room with Linda on your upcoming trip. Until you are married, I strongly counsel you to arrange two separate rooms— always, not just on this trip, and not just with Linda. You are responsible for protecting the well-being of any woman and the purity of your relationship with her. Let the sharing of a single room wait until marriage, when it will further symbolize the shared privacy of a one-flesh union.
>
> I know you and Linda have talked about proper control in expressing your affection, so you certainly recognize that as an issue of sober consequence. The apostle Paul wrote earnestly to Timothy, his youthful son in the faith, on the same issue. His counsel? *Flee such desires.* Don't indulge them. Don't even talk them out. *Run away* from the very presence of temptation. *Two* rooms!
>
> Seek the highest and best. Do not make financial thrift a reason to expose Linda and yourself to unwise romantic temptations. Regard this trip a date with a friend, not a taste of marriage.
>
> I want to invest in your godliness through the enclosed $300 check for a second room. If it costs more and you cannot raise it, let me know and I will provide the funds. . . . Love, Mom.

This godly mother did not just sigh in resignation about the lax morality of today's society. Others in her generation might merely say, "What's the use? Times have changed. Since our kids are going to have sex anyway, we might as well just provide for birth control and protection against disease." Such defeatist statements do not sound like "the salt of the earth" we are expected to be. Salt is *intrusive.* It makes its presence felt in a recipe, serving to bring out the robust flavor of each unique ingredient. This mother knew she could not force her son into godly morality, but she could urge him into it by offering sound, rational arguments and removing a financial roadblock.

Teaching from the Behavior of Others

A couple we know used a family dilemma to teach their teenaged daughter and two adult sons a high view of marriage. The wife's side of the family had an annual tradition of gathering every Memorial Day, with a different sibling hosting each year.

One year the wife's sister, Carol, was to hold the family reunion at her home in St. Louis, where she lived with her boyfriend, Conrad. Our friends at first debated whether or not to go, but they finally decided to attend, as an expression of family solidarity. To keep this from appearing as a tacit endorsement of cohabitation outside marriage, they wrote an explanatory letter to their children. A shortened version appears below:

We have decided to accept Carol's invitation because we love her, but we remain uncertain about how to conduct ourselves toward her and Conrad. Since they seem to be asking us to celebrate with them a relationship that is *not* a marriage, we want to clarify our views on this matter.

Whenever we attend wedding ceremonies, we take to heart these words: "Marriage is ordained by God and to be held in high esteem by all men." For a man and woman to live together—without establishing a legal union by taking public vows—is to hold marriage in low esteem. This relationship is not the same as *holy* matrimony, since "holy" means "special, uncommon, set aside for the honor and worship of God." Living together without marriage states that marriage is not special and sacred, that long-term commitment doesn't matter.

Because Carol and Conrad have not asked God to join them together, we see them illegitimately stealing a one-flesh relationship in disregard of God's commands. We would like to influence them toward reverence for God and a personal surrender to Christ as Lord of their lives. We are not yet sure how to do that, but we know we must keep lines of communication open with them to have any influence. So, we will go to the Memorial Day festivities. We look forward to seeing you there. Love, Mom and Dad.

Personalized Wedding Vows

We once attended a wedding in which the ceremony opened with a groomsman carrying in a banner proclaiming that verse from the lips of Joshua: " . . . as for me and my house, we will serve the LORD" (Josh. 24:15 KJV). The spectacle so electrified us that we later borrowed that banner from the bride's family. Dennis proudly carried it in to initiate the pageantry of our son David's wedding to Brenda Shrock.

David and Brenda's wedding ceremony moved everyone present because of the deeply personal nature of their vows. The bride and groom earnestly looked into each other's eyes as they said from memory words they had written to pledge their mutual commitment. With their permission we reproduce their vows here:

DAVID: Brenda, I am giving my life to you! With the blessing of our families and friends and of God our Father, I promise to share with you all my thoughts, all my dreams, and all my love for all my life!

You have become my best friend, my favorite person. I cherish you above all others because God has brought us together and He is allowing us to be married so we can share the closest, most wonderful friendship of all. I count my love for you the same as my love for Christ because both are my highest calling in life. I am loving my Lord by loving you with all my heart, all my soul, and all my might!

I will be your companion in everything. Especially with our wonderful differences, you have become such a great treasure to me. Our companionship in all of life fulfills and completes me. I believe we will discover God's heart more closely as we grow in sharing and understanding each other's heart.

I will be completely yours through success and failure, sickness and health, joy and sorrow, prosperity and "lean times," confidence and uncertainty, frustration and disappointment, inspiration and celebration! I will always talk about everything with you, always express my thoughts and feelings, always overcome misunderstanding, always heal hurts, always forgive and ask forgiveness, remind and remember, explain and affirm, restore and renew!

Brenda, I promise to cherish, care for, and encourage you as we grow together in the spirit of our Lord Jesus all the days of our lives!

BRENDA: Dave, I am giving my life to you with the blessing of our family and friends and of God our Father. I commit to you all my heart, all my thoughts, all my dreams, and all my love.

I will cherish you and our life together above all else. I will always trust, always hope, and always believe in you. Dave, I will always be there for you if you need encouragement, advice, laughter, or someone to share your tears. I always want to be your best friend.

I am committed to praying for you and with you as we seek God's plan for our lives.

I will honor, respect, and esteem you, submitting to your loving leadership.

You have my heart, Dave, unbelievably in the same way Christ does. Dave, I promise to care for and love you as we grow together in the spirit of our Lord Jesus all the days of our lives.

We always take our attendance at a wedding ceremony as an obligation to hold the couple in future days to the vows they made on that wedding day. Why else have witnesses? In our day the tradition of inviting guests has degenerated to a meaningless form, a mere social gesture or time of entertainment.

We would like to see ceremonies include, preferably from the bride and groom themselves, a specific request to all in attendance. It might sound something like this:

"We hereby authorize you to hold us to these vows if at any future time you hear that either of us is departing from them."

Vows *Before* Marriage

Several sets of parents have inspired us recently by telling of covenants they made with their teenage sons and daughters. After the parents have explained human sexuality, including God's design for its sublime pleasure in marriage and the threats to its purity in modern society, they invite their children to make a vow of premarital chastity.

One couple with four children has added a special touch—a ring for each child to wear until his or her wedding day. That child will later present the ring to the marriage partner as a symbolic gift of his or her virginity. (This family's story appeared in a published article: Richard Durfield, "A Promise with a Ring to It" [*Focus on the Family*, April 1990, pp. 2–4]).

An Afterword

All parents hope for happy marriages for their children. We do well if we can so guide them in their growing-up years that they will choose a lifetime partner of whom we approve and can lovingly welcome into our family. Sometimes, however, we cannot wholeheartedly give our blessings to the union because we object to either the intended mate or the timing and "practicalities" of the marriage. Most likely the wedding will take place anyhow, in which case your child may be painfully sandwiched between warring factions: parents and the person he or she has promised to cherish above all others.

If you have a son or daughter who plans to marry without your consent, examine your motives very carefully. Are you being fair and truly objective? Do you really know the person your child wants you to accept? Perhaps you are merely finding it hard to relinquish your previous role as the most important person in your child's life. If, indeed, there are specific reasons for your disapproval, point them out calmly and try to forestall the wedding plans, at least temporarily. That may not work! If the couple does marry, attend the ceremony and later give them your wholehearted support in making the marriage succeed. Let there be no "I told you so!" if the union seems to be faltering. Rather, hold your child accountable for the commitment he or she has made before God and the world. (See also, "Marital Stresses of Adult Children" in chapter 5.)

5

Counseling Opportunities

Dennis

"Counseling" involves dispensing advice, instruction, and encouragement, sometimes all at the same time. When your children ask for your guidance, they are temporarily surrendering part of themselves—in effect trusting you to hold them *accountable* for their behavioral choices. It is a lot tougher to counsel someone who has not invited your intervention, but there are some basic principles to remember in either situation.

Accountability

For the past few years I have made myself regularly "accountable" to two other Christian men. I call one of them every Tuesday morning at six o'clock. The other calls me once a month, at noon on a Thursday. Each of my counselors asks me questions from a list that I have prepared. These represent disciplines that I want to continually cultivate in my life.

The weekly calls focus on a short consistent list; the monthly calls feature probing questions from a large pool of topics. Some examples follow:

Marriage: "What did you do to cherish your wife yesterday?"

Bible study: "Since we talked last, on how many of the days did you do the daily reading you planned?"

Wisdom: "What is the latest nugget you have gleaned from your Bible reading or meditation?"

Financial freedom: "What steps have you taken toward or away from your goal since our last talk?"

Self-control: "Tell me a recent occasion in which you began to magnify some negative emotion, and how you handled it."

Time use: "Give me an example of poor efficiency in the past week and what you would do differently now."

Reading: "What are you currently reading besides Scripture? What are you learning from it?"

This arrangement to give regular accountings allows me to say, "I myself am a man under authority." Jesus praised a Roman centurion who spoke these words (Matt. 8:9). He understood how to *exercise* authority because he knew how to function *under* it.

In the New Testament we detect the apostle Paul's exercise of authority over his son in the faith, Timothy. In turn, Timothy exercised authority over elders in the church at Ephesus. By my regular phone calls, I take the role of Timothy: I place myself under the men who take the role of Paul in holding me accountable. I can also function as Paul when my own sons take the role of Timothy in phone calls where they give an accounting to me. For example, my sons have asked me to quiz them on such questions as the following:

"What are you doing to develop your confidence in public speaking?"

"What have you done in the past week to practice starting conversations with strangers?"

"Tell me an instance in the past week in which you responded respectfully to unfair treatment from your employer. How are you coming along in balancing assertiveness with thoughtfulness?"

Building on Strengths

In a phone call to one of our sons, I found occasion to use a counseling technique described in my book *Vitality Therapy* (Grand Rapids: Baker, 1989). This book features dozens of practical techniques that *nonprofessional* counselors can use to make maximum use of brief counseling opportunities. In that phone call I helped David transfer a skill from one area of his life to an area in which he was experiencing difficulty.

Knowing that this conscientious son had just begun a new job over which he fretted, I asked, "When you worry over your work, how would you describe the worry and the pressure you feel?" Dave answered, "I look at all the various things I have to do and think to myself, 'It's too big for me.' "

Since I already knew that he excelled at his favorite recreation—technical rock climbing—I asked, "Dave, when you're out rock climbing, do you ever stand at the foot of a sheer cliff hundreds of feet high, look up at it, and say to yourself, 'It's too big for me'?" I thought he would answer "Yes." Then I would ask him how he managed to enjoy the sport anyway, implying that he could use the same kind of attitude toward on-the-job chores. However, to my surprise, David answered quickly and confidently, "Never!" I commented, "Wow, that's amazing! How do you work up the confidence for such a demanding task?"

The climber's answer came back, "I always know I can

get around any tough move on a climb just by putting out a sudden burst of more energy."

I then helped him transfer his success in the area of climbing to that of job responsibilities: "How can you apply the more-energy principle to the mountain of demands you face on your job?"

David paused on the other end of the line, then pondered, "Hmm, the more-energy principle. I never looked at it that way before, but I *could* view any difficulty in life as just another kind of rock climb. And I already *know* I can handle that. Hmm. I'll have to think about that."

The next week on the phone Dave reported, "Dad, I've had a great week with my job. Every time I face something that seems too big for me, a phrase pops into my mind: 'more-energy principle.' Then I just put out an extra burst and *handle* it. Like, if I have a talk to give in front of some people, I feel scared at first, but then I just say to myself, 'I can hardly wait to give this talk!' Doing that makes me feel enthusiastic instead of worried—just like when I'm climbing."

We can help our sons and daughters solve current problems that discourage them by bringing to their attention some ways they have already solved other problems. Suppose a son faces weeks of tedious work to qualify for a higher position and does not think he can stand the monotony. You recall that he suffered through weeks of boredom while recovering from a serious illness in fourth grade. If you ask him how he managed *that* rough time, you help him access a solution to a *job* problem that he has unconsciously categorized as a solution to a *medical* matter.

Wisdom by Example

The summer I turned fourteen, I had a summer-camp counselor named Dave Russell. Dave daily taught us boys in Mohawk cabin that Jesus Christ was a gentleman. Dave claimed Jesus as the Lord of his life and recommended that we boys do the same. He urged us to show the kind of courtesy to others that Jesus did. When the dinner bell rang and other kids pushed and shoved to get into the dining hall first, the men of Mohawk cabin were to hold back and walk in *last*. Dave taught us a specific example of Philippians 2:3–4—to put other people's interests ahead of our own.

One day Mohawk cabin went out canoeing and I had a chance to see Dave Russell put his money where his mouth was. My partner and I were making it all right on the narrow, twisting Deerskin River. But Dave was having trouble in the canoe ahead because he had in the bow the clumsiest kid in camp, Wally. When they got their canoe stuck sideways in the stream, Dave tried patiently to tell Wally what to do to get them going again. He told Wally to lift his paddle from the left side of the canoe and put it into the water on the right-hand side.

Most guys would have simply moved that paddle from one side to the other *in front* of them. Not Wally. To avoid some brush in front of him, he lifted the paddle high over his head behind him. As he reached for the paddle's handle with his right hand, he missed it. It slipped out of his grasp, and the flat blade of the paddle fell smack on the top of Dave's head. To this day I can still hear the "thwock" sound it made.

In a situation like this, every man I had ever known before would blow up in anger and burst out with a string of profanity. I felt sure that Dave would, too, as I watched red color rise up his neck and fill his cheeks.

But Dave surprised me. When he drew the breath that I thought would erupt in yelling, Dave paused a second, controlled himself, then said gently, "Come on, Wally. Let's try again." And I never forgot this example of a man of God showing that valuable fruit of the Spirit: patient self-control. When feeling aggravated, I now often remind myself, "I'm one of Dave Russell's boys."

Dave did not know that someone was watching him. He did not stop to think that a scrawny camper would someday write about his actions for thousands of people to read. He simply followed the example of Jesus, his Lord—the gentleman. Without Dave Russell's influence, I might not be writing a *Christian* book today. It was at a particular bend of the Deerskin River on an ordinary August afternoon that Dave passed a crucial test. That action opened a young camper's mind to the message Dave *said* mattered most to him.

"Kids" of all ages continue to study those of us who claim to follow Christ. The example we set affects people more than what we say. You can count on it—*someone* is watching, perhaps your *own* kid.

Counseling Through Affirmation

Ruth and I have created several ways to invest in our sons' lives as they grew up. One example is celebrating a monthly "special day" for each member of our family. This started a tradition that we have continued even after our sons have left our nest. The very fact that this tradition regularly re-affirms our family ties makes it part of an ongoing support system that sometimes provides an opportunity for counseling.

During our boys' late grade school years, we began a custom we called "V.I.P. Day." (A V.I.P. of course, is a "Very Important Person.") Each family member had one such day per month—the day of the month on which the person was born. For example, because Steve was born on September 3, the third of *every* month was "Steven Day" in our house. Because Ruth was born on May 25, we celebrate the twenty-fifth of *every* month.

We enjoyed many novel ways of celebrating these special occasions. Usually we did something as low key as just announcing around the breakfast table, "Hey, today is 'David Day'!" Then we would wish the honoree a happy day and tell why he (or she) was a very important person to us. Other times, family members might offer a back rub to the V.I.P. Or perhaps the V.I.P. could choose some kind of inexpensive activity, such as breakfast out with Dad. Other times there was a list of available activities from which to choose.

We still acknowledge V.I.P. Day to each of our boys, even though they now live far away in homes of their own. We make a phone call or write a letter wishing them a happy day. This provides a vehicle for keeping open the lines of rapport and blessing. A written format enables us to include some affirming words of counsel and to strengthen our sons' godly character traits, but even a phone call can convey loving encouragement.

Learning from Grandparents

Children can discover either positive or negative role models in their grandparents, and we parents can use either example to teach wisdom. On the positive side, a mother might tell her kids something like this: "I so much appreciated Grandma's thoughtfulness today. When I got home from work tired, she asked me how my day went. She gave me the chance to unload mentally— without interrupting. She's really good at that."

On the negative side, we heard of one couple who lived with the husband's divorced mother in a house they owned jointly with her. (This often creates special problems!) Grandma began having men spend the night in her room with her. The couple confronted Grandma by pointing out that her actions were not right and did not set a godly example for her grandchildren. They insisted that if she did not change her actions, either she or they would have to move elsewhere, no matter how many complications this would cause.

This sandwiched couple used a tense issue to teach their children the biblical principles of moral purity. They first explained the meaning of the words *fornication* and *adultery* at a level the kids could understand. They then said, "We love Grandma, but in this case she is doing something wrong. We cannot act as if it does not matter to us, because it matters to God and we honor him as the Lord of our lives. Many people in our day would say that it is up to Mom what she does sexually. We don't agree, but we cannot control her conduct; that is *her* business. However, we do not have to consent to her use of our home for ungodly purposes." In all of this ordeal they treated Grandma respectfully. They honored her *position* while opposing her *conduct.*

Marital Stresses of Adult Children

We recently were with a wonderful group of people who occupy the upper end of the sandwich years. They seemed to have gained a whole new freedom to accept themselves and their spouses as they were. They averaged about sixty years of age. Although they showed fun and vital, youthful qualities on the outside, when we spoke with them personally we discovered a great deal of hidden pain over the wounded marriages of their adult children, who had been married from one to fifteen years.

These parents were hurting over not only the fact that the young people had stresses in their marriages, but also that the kids looked on divorce as an easy escape from the tension. Years before, the parents hardly considered divorce an option when facing their own stresses. They *learned* to cope, to adapt and get along with each other. Many changed their expectations or flexed in other ways that allowed their marriages to continue. They were heartbroken on hearing their children say such defeatist sentences as, "I can't live with this kind of unhappiness. We're incompatible."

What can parents do in such situations? At the least, they can refuse to give their ready endorsement of marital breakup. More than that, they can encourage the young spouses to work out their differences. One young wife got fed up with her inattentive husband and went "home" to stay with her beloved mom and dad. They immediately told her to take her luggage and go right back to her husband to try to work out the problems with him. They reassured her that they loved her. But they would not let their home serve as an escape from her responsibilities as a wife.

Of course, if spousal abuse is involved, parents should provide at least a temporary sanctuary for their children and grandchildren until legal action is possible. Otherwise, the parents' efforts should focus on providing emotional support and a sympathetic ear. Since parents are usually privy to only one part of the total picture, they may find it hard to be objective. They may also be unfairly judgmental, taking the side of one party (usually their own child's). If only for that reason, they may best serve the interests of all if they encourage a son or daughter in a faltering marriage to seek professional counseling in hopes of salvaging the union.

Parents can find marital wisdom by reading certain books and might also recommend some on the following list to their troubled children:

Gibson, Dennis L. *The Strong-Willed Adult.* Grand Rapids, Baker Book House, 1987. (Focuses on self-discipline. Includes a section on how to live with "difficult" loved ones.)

Jenkins, Jerry. *Hedges.* Brentwood, Tenn. Wolgemuth & Hyatt, 1989. (Subtitle: *Loving Your Marriage Enough to Protect It.* Contains practical ways to ensure sexual fidelity.)

Schwambach, Stephen. *Tough Talk to a Stubborn Spouse.* Eugene, Oreg.: Harvest House, 1990. (Blunt, humorous words to anyone thinking of divorce. Answers all the excuses with godly common sense.)

Williams, Pat, and Jenkins, Jerry B. *Rekindled.* Old Tappan, N.J.: Revell, 1985. (Describes a marriage with the love "all gone," then built again from the pits.)

An Afterword

One scarcely needs a professional degree to be a counselor, in the broadest sense of the word. Much that we do as parents falls into that category. Although dispensing advice may seem relatively straightforward when our children are young, it requires a much more delicate approach once they have become adults.

If you have established the right kind of relationship with them during their growing years, your children will probably continue to welcome your input throughout their lives. However, remember not to push! They are now independent adults (at least we hope so), which means you no longer have control of what they do and what choices they make. But "be there" for them—always.

Part Two

Parents
to
Our Parents

6

"Honor Your Father and Mother"

Ruth

As Dennis's parents reached their seventies, he realized that he would not always have an opportunity to tell them everything he wanted them to know. So he scheduled a special time to meet with them, even though they lived apart. Then he made it a point to ask their forgiveness for all the items he could think of that he had never before cleaned up with them. Even more important, he concentrated on thanking them for specific precious memories. For example, he thanked his father for this memory:

Dad, I remember one time when I was about three or four years old. You were sitting in your favorite chair in our living room, reading the newspaper. I was pretending to run our vacuum cleaner. The cord was coiled up on the handle and not plugged in, and I was just making believe.

I remember that you put down your newspaper and looked at me with a warm, gentle smile. You said kindly, "Den, why don't you uncoil the cord, plug it in, turn on the switch, and *really* vacuum?" Dad, you can't believe how proud it made me to know that my dad thought I could do useful work.

Dennis's father, his eyes glistening, answered, "I don't remember that occasion, Den, but thank you so much for telling me." A few months later the whole Gibson family gathered for Thanksgiving. As was customary, we spent a large part of the time reminiscing. During a lull in the conversation, Dennis's dad spoke up. "Den," he asked, "do you remember the time you were a little kid pretending to vacuum and I told you to plug in the cord and *really vacuum?*" Dennis held back his tears and answered simply, "I sure do, Dad."

Dennis and I looked across the room at each other, realizing what had just happened. The happy memory that had once eluded Dennis's dad became his again when Dennis told it to him several weeks before. What a fine way to honor a parent! Especially if we have had difficulties with them, what a way to fulfill Jesus' commandment to love those who have offended us!

Showing Your Love *Now*

One way we can respect and love our parents is to review with them our fond memories of their own best actions in the past. Things we tell them that we appreciate from our childhoods enter their minds and hearts and become their own memories, enriching their present days in the process.

At a person's funeral, family and friends gather around and share their precious memories about the departed loved one. Someone usually gives a eulogy, literally a "good speech." We believe those good words should be spoken while our loved ones can still hear them.

Sit down before it's too late and think of two or three

specific, *positive* memories about each of your parents. Then go to them, or at least write, and tell them these memories. Emphasize how much the experiences meant to you at the time. Add no qualifying statements like, "I sure wish you would have done it more often" or, "Don't think that outweighs all the bad things." Keep your message as a love gift to your parent.

Let there be no later regrets regarding *any* loved one. Make sure *now* that you say everything you will wish you had said if that person should die suddenly today. Keep up to date. Let every good-bye serve well enough as the last, if it must be. Spare yourself from saying then, "Oh, how I wish I had. . . ."

Loving the Unlovely

Dennis did not consider his father the kind of man that he would choose as an adult companion. Dad was often coarse, profane, and irritable. Therefore, since Dennis did not *like* many of his father's qualities, he *loved* him. Love involves a decision. That means Dennis did the specific kinds of things he would have done if he actually felt a great fondness for his father.

During the last three years of his life, Dennis's father, Murray, lived alone in a one-room apartment. He remained alienated from his wife (Dennis's mother) and seldom had visits from friends. Dennis's three younger brothers lived hundreds of miles away and called Dad several times a month. We made it a point to visit with Murray twice a month. Typically the three of us went out to lunch at a Chinese restaurant. Murray always chuckled at the item "beef kow" on the Cantonese-cuisine menu: "What other kind of cow could you find than a beef cow?" That memory now stands as a reminder to us of Murray's whimsical side and a way we can still honor him in our hearts.

When Dennis talked with his father every few days on the phone, he always ended each conversation by saying,

"I love you, Dad." He was not necessarily reporting his feelings but stating his intentions. Later, Dennis found a tangible way to love his father in his last days in the hospital. When Murray had trouble breathing, Dennis would help him with an inhalation exercise. This required Murray to cough up sputum which Dennis would catch in a towel he held under Dad's chin. During this operation, Dennis could coach, "Atta boy, Dad! Get it up! You can do it." When we love, we choose to affirm another's personhood and encourage his or her efforts.

Celebrating as a Family

My own parents, Eric and Ruth Flesvig, were able to celebrate fifty-two years of married life together. As a preschooler, I used to love it when my family left together on a trip in our maroon 1940 Chevy and Daddy launched into singing,

"Put on your old gray bonnet with the blue ribbon on it,
  While I hitch old Dobbin to the shay.
And through the fields of clover, we'll ride up to Dover,
  On our golden wedding day."

The older I got, and the more Mom and Dad sang "their" song, the more I looked forward to helping them celebrate their fiftieth wedding anniversary. I vowed I would somehow "hitch old Dobbin to the shay" for them on that fine day. So, when that golden anniversary finally did come, I secretly arranged for a horse and buggy to pick them up at their home.

Dennis had dubbed a cassette tape from a record of Mitch Miller and his gang singing "Put On Your Old Gray Bonnet." As the half-century pair came out of their building, he played it over and over again. We now hear it in the background whenever we watch our videotape of the occasion. It shows people cheering the Flesvigs, shaking their hands, and patting them on the back. And it captures that priceless moment of surprise when they glimpsed their special transportation.

The honored pair invited their children into the shay with them for the two-mile trip to a meeting place I had arranged. There, friends and relatives gathered for a time of eating, sharing, watching a slide show, and appreciating the Flesvigs with their stories of fond memories. I read congratulatory telegrams from the mayor of the town, the governor of the state, and even the President of the United States. How heartwarming it was to hear government officials express their support for marital solidarity because they know it forms the foundation for our nation's vitality.

Dennis honored my parents in a speech at the ceremony. He confessed to the audience why he had never acted on his occasional impulses to "just run away to the woods somewhere." He feared that his father-in-law would come after him, grab him by the scruff of the neck, and drag him back home! Eric Flesvig—upholder of integrity.

We all learned some golden lessons that day:

1. If you find yourself fortunate enough to have relatives who reach a fifieth wedding anniversary, by all means make a big deal of it. Celebrate your joy as a family.
2. Let the very idea of it inspire you to reach your own golden wedding day.
3. Set the example of a solid heritage of commitment for the children and grandchildren who are watching.
4. Plan the celebration with three generations in mind: the *older*, who set the example; the *middle*, who need to support it; and the *younger*, who are forming the values that will guide their endurance through the "worse" of the for-better-or-for-worse days of married life.
5. Document the occasion. Make video cassettes and audio tapes. Take pictures. Have a local newspaper

reporter and photographer there. "Make history"—
and make it good.

Preserving Tradition

Eric Flesvig, my dad, followed a charming ritual after
every meal he ate with family members. He would lay
down his napkin and say, "Well, I've had many a meal in
my day. . . ." Just the unfinished statement served as his
trademark for a compliment. Occasionally he gave the
full version, particularly if the meal had some obvious
defect: " . . . but I've never had one quite like this." He
said all this with a characteristic boyish grin that sur-
vives on our favorite photograph of him.

Traditions and rituals function as the threads that
stitch together the fabric of a family. I always loved the
annual Christmas Eve smorgasbord that my Swedish
mother's side of the family arranged. To this day we continue it, long after the generation that introduced us to it
can no longer shepherd the preparations or be present.

We started a tradition with our own three sons in their
late teens. We call it "The Annual Cultural Event." On
some evening during the Christmas season we all go to a
dinner theater for a meal followed by some classic play.
(*The Music Man* holds first place in our affection, partly
because it inaugurated this family tradition.)

Marking a Passage

In the summer following his freshman year of college,
Dennis helped his mother and brothers move into a small
house. For twenty-nine years the family affectionately
referred to that house as "605," its street address. During
that era it stood as the Gibson household, captained by
Dennis's divorced mother, Marguerite. It served as the
nest from which Dennis's three younger brothers finished
their grade school and high school years.

Finally a day came when Marguerite could no longer
manage the upkeep and decided to move to a small apart-

ment. At age seventy-four she sold "605." We helped her gradually move her possessions, some to her apartment, some to our house. The new people moved in—a single mother with three young boys—history repeating itself within those walls.

We recall the day we went with Grandma Gibson to remove the last armload of her belongings from the old homestead and to celebrate the last good-bye. Dennis gathered the adults into a circle and said, "People, let's pray our thanks for what this house has meant to one generation and what it shall mean to a new one." He concluded, "You have been a good house, 605. And, Great God, creator of all things, you have taken delight in the laughter that saturates these walls. We thank you for the years and memories that have been and for those yet to come here at 605. It has been good. It was lived as we pray, in the name of Jesus. Amen."

This brief ceremony put a punctuation mark at the end of one paragraph of life. It honored the tiny woman under Dennis's right arm who had given her earnest best to those twenty-nine years and to that edifice. She could now move on to her new living quarters with a sense of closure because she had the opportunity to say good-bye. Loved ones had shared that farewell with her, lingering over it and acknowledging that the past was very good— and past.

By contrast, we know of another family where a daughter did not believe in sentiment. In a curt, businesslike way, she rushed her mother out of the old family home. That mother felt unfinished with her beloved past attachments and had a hard time adjusting to her new living quarters. She often spoke to another daughter of her nervousness that she might offend the one who had "rushed" her.

Help a parent view the leaving of a home as a graduation, a fresh beginning. Make it a commencement celebration, moving on to the new, on the solid base of a past *you* have declared "good."

Ease the adjustment period—but don't insist on being appreciated! A friend of ours recently helped his mother mount some shelf brackets on the walls of her new apartment. He spent two laborious hours on finding the studs, drilling into them, and fitting the brackets with just the right-size screws. Later that day his sister stopped by the apartment with some boards that she placed on the brackets in about five minutes.

For weeks the mother talked about how hard her *daughter* worked in putting up the boards! Her son told us he held his tongue when he felt like protesting. He paraphrased a scriptural insight as follows: "Thou shalt not insist on getting credit."

The son needed an extra shot of grace in the moments when he envied Mom's unbalanced praise toward his sister. He stood at a crossroad each time he heard Mom extol Sis. He chose to use these gracious words: "It sure is nice to know your daughter looks after you, isn't it, Mom?" He realized it mattered keenly to Mom that she and her daughter live on good terms, especially since they had some rocky years between them during the girl's adolescence.

Practicing Simple Courtesies

One day Dennis and I took my mother to a fine restaurant to celebrate her birthday. After the main course, the waitress came to clear our table. She asked me about my mother, "Is she done?" Mother is not deaf or incapable, so I deliberately asked, "Mom, are you done?"

The waitress had addressed the generation with which she could best relate. We see this also when people encounter a mother carrying a toddler in her arms or a father walking with his five-year-old along the hall at church. People talk *about* these kids, in their presence, as if the youngsters have no identity or capability. Even if you have reason to think they cannot hear or understand you, talk to young and old as if they count with you as individuals.

Sometimes the younger generation can help us remember to respect them. I once attended a slide show at a friend's house with our youngest son, then about twenty. While chatting over coffee, a woman I did not know very well looked at me and asked about our son. "How old is he?" He was sitting next to me and gracefully eased that awkward moment by quipping gently, "Why don't we ask him?" All three of our boys now use that reply with us whenever we ask one about the activities or opinions of another.

I periodically visit a friend's mother in a nursing home. Although the woman has not talked in fifteen years, I still talk to her with respect. On some level it *might* penetrate. We tend to create a Twilight Zone experience of nonexistence for people when we talk *about* them in their presence. We act as if a plastic bubble separates them from us. I know that just because they don't give a signal back does not mean they are not hearing, so I sometimes sing to the old woman or quote a Scripture verse to her.

An Afterword

The apostle Paul gives the commandment-with-a-promise in Ephesians as part of his teaching about *family* living. Therefore, we take it to guide our "honoring" attitudes toward mother and father, toward our relatives on both sides of the generational sandwich, and toward other fellow members of the human family.

7

A Little Goes a Long Way

Dennis

Act One

One morning Ruth took her eighty-one-year-old mother to visit her sister (Ruth's Aunt Edith) at The Holmstad, a nearby retirement community. At 9:15 they arrived at Edith's lovely studio apartment, where Edith gave Ruth two large plastic bags of used clothing. She intended these for the Repeat Boutique, a place in our community where missionaries, refugees, and foreign students can get good clothing free of charge. Then Ruth's mother gave Edith an important paper she had wanted to deliver.

Ruth then helped the women into the car. The two older women commented on *how much they had already accomplished that day.* Ruth drove to a familiar department store in a nearby mall. Edith bought a small hand vacuum cleaner. Ruth's mom bought a box of facial tissues. While they were shopping, Ruth purchased a pair of shoes. About twenty minutes had elapsed.

The trio left the shopping center, with the two sisters commenting once again on *how much they had accomplished that day*, adding that they never could have done it without Ruth. It was still early, only 10:15 A.M.

Act Two

A Young Widow, Old with Alzheimer's

The three returned to The Holmstad to visit Ruth's beloved cousin, Lois. Although only fifty-seven, Lois had suffered for years with Alzheimer's disease. She functioned about like a one-year-old—and not a happy one-year-old at that.

Lois had been Ruth's teenage idol, a beautiful high school girl who introduced Ruth to Bing Crosby's immortal rendition of "White Christmas" in the 1940s. As a lively teenager who loved to dance, she often wore a white skirt with the names "Perry Como" and "Frank Sinatra" and other popular singers of the day carefully embroidered into the fabric.

That day, Lois sat in the "Alzheimer chair" in comfortable leisurewear that her visitors knew covered the diaper fastened underneath. She drooled down her front. Her loved ones could not get her to recognize them. Lois, who once owned more perfume bottles than Ruth had ever seen outside a department store, now had a sour odor about her. Ruth had not seen her cousin for several months and found it hard to accept her deterioration.

Not What She Used to Be

Then Ruth and the others went to another room to see her oldest aunt, Ann, who had just had surgery on a drooping eyelid. Ruth could not visit for long because of Ann's discomfort and need to sleep. Ruth remembered this eighty-seven-year-old in her prime, forty-some years earlier, when Ann earned her living making beautiful lampshades in her home in Chicago.

Ruth left Ann after giving her the simple pleasure of some chocolate-chip cookies. Edith gave Ann a new box of tissues. On the way to the car Edith and Ruth's mom talked again about *how much they had accomplished that day.* It was not yet 11:00 A.M.

Routine Errands

A short drive took the three to Edith's dentist, who removed the plaque from her false teeth and checked her gums for irritations. The women loved the way the kind dentist took time to recommend fun restaurants for their lunch. (Note to any professionals reading this: small, friendly gestures like that generate volumes of goodwill.)

Out of several fine restaurant options, Ruth's mom and Edith chose McDonald's. That day the golden arches featured a special test-market hamburger with cheese, onions, and a wheat bun. The ladies proclaimed it the best they had ever tasted. As they left, the sisters agreed that they had *certainly accomplished more than they could have imagined that day.*

The next stop was to be Edith's bank. Edith had always known her way around the area quite well and could capably tell a driver which way to go. So Ruth let Edith guide, often asking her, "Left or right?" Only a year or two earlier on such trips Edith would have answered with the word *left* or *right.* This day though, she merely gestured one way or the other with a wave of her hand, saying, "That way." When Ruth asked why she did that, Edith admitted that she could no longer call out the direction with assurance, even though she still knew she wrote with her *right* hand. Ruth also recognized that in her own early fifties she forgot certain mechanical tasks if she had not done them in a long time. For example, what numbers should she use if she wanted to put her telephone on "Call Forward"?

They drove up to a remote teller machine and stuck the check into a metal slot. A young woman behind a glass about eight yards away spoke to them through a loudspeaker. Both Ruth's mom and Edith said they would not have wanted to do that transaction if they could not have *seen* the teller.

At the end of their four-hour time together, the two older women again remarked that they *had accomplished so much that day.* It was barely 1:00 P.M.

What Ruth Learned

As Ruth reviewed the events of that morning, she concluded several things about the elderly:

1. Accomplishing specific tasks gives them a sense of success and being in control. They know they are alive.
2. By repeating any fact, they reassure each other of its truth.
3. It takes only a little accomplishment to generate substantial feelings of contentment.
4. Even a little kindness goes a long way, whatever our age.
5. We of the next-younger generation differ from the elderly only in degree. We merely pack more activities into our hours (and sometimes accomplish little).
6. In the middle of the sandwich, we do well to quiz ourselves. Which really benefits us more: (a) doing a few things and feeling great about them; or (b) doing many things and feeling pressured or dissatisfied about them?

An Afterword

Tending to our elderly parents and relatives offers us not a burden but an opportunity to show our love. I have appreciated the way Ruth has wholeheartedly given herself to these widows. She doesn't roll her eyes or sigh at the one inconvenience after another that their disabilities bring her way. Nor does she complain resentfully, "I have to go again to visit them."

At the end of the first chapter of his earnest letter to fellow Christians, James said, "Religion that God our Father accepts as pure and faultless is this: to look after orphans and widows in their distress, and to keep oneself from being polluted by the world." I think those two ideas go together. One way to keep ourselves from the seductions of advertising and our own covetousness is to give ourselves away to needy people. I see Ruth living that pure religion and reaping the joyful benefit of the commandment-with-a-promise, as she honors her elders. A little love goes a long way.

Failing Capabilities

Dennis

Great Aunt Sabrina, age eighty-four, kept forgetting where she put her checkbook. Her nephew helped with her finances, but the old woman felt secure knowing she had access to that checkbook, though she often misplaced it and could not remember where. Sometimes she left it on the hall table in her apartment. Sometimes it turned up in her top dresser drawer or in the desk.

Although Aunt Sabrina lived alone, once a day a younger woman came to bring groceries, prepare a meal, and make sure of Sabrina's well-being. The nephew paid the young woman for three hours a day of home care. However, she soon began to show impatience with Sabrina's forgetfulness. The caregiver reported to the nephew that she would have to "teach Sabrina a lesson." She felt compelled to "spell it out to her" and to discipline the old woman for forgetting simple things. The young worker's irritable attitude created such stress for Sabrina that the nephew had to find a replacement.

The Need for Patience

Working with the elderly calls for full-time patience and respect. Whenever we treat them like naughty children, we disobey the spirit of the commandment to "honor father and mother." This honoring attitude toward the generation ahead of us reflects our reverence toward our divine Father in heaven whose name we hallow.

Answer Each Time as If It Were the First

When the elderly ask the same question over and over, we can answer in a kind and gentle manner as if they are asking it for the first time. Suppose that you pick up your father to take him to the dental appointment as he had requested. On the way he asks you three times, "Where are you taking me?" Answer *each* time brightly, "To your dentist. You have an appointment today." Don't add even the word *Remember?* Don't sigh at the third repetition and blurt out disgustedly, "Dad, that's the third time you've asked me the same question." Do not emotionally spank Dad with a loaded interrogation like, "Now what did I just tell you?"

Welcome every opportunity to administer unconditional love to a faltering loved one, even as Christ has given us grace in spite of our imperfections. When we deal with the inconveniences of caring for the elderly, we extend Christ's helping hands to them. Our verbal patience will steady them as they stumble.

"Consider It Pure Joy"

Remember, when you answer your aging parents' questions, change their diapers, or shop for them, *they once did these things for you.* "A cheerful heart is good medicine" (Prov. 17:23) as it transfers your strength to another. Do not complain, even if you face such intimate tasks as giving bed baths, washing soiled laundry, or changing a colostomy bag. Be grateful for the opportunity to serve the older generation. You may someday need the same kind of caregiving. May you be fortunate enough to have the kind of loving descendants we urge *you* to be.

Many elderly people feel lonely, neglected, and out of the mainstream of life, simply because their field of activity or circle of friends has narrowed. For those living in retirement communites or who have given up driving, a weekly outing comes as a great blessing. "But how can I do that when I have so many other obligations?" you ask. Think about it. What will you wish you had done when you stand someday at the graveside of that loved one? Do it *now*. The time grows short, and you will not be "inconvenienced" for long. You will never again have *this* opportunity to give a cup of cold water to *this* representative of a thirsty Jesus, who said, " . . . whatever you did for one of the least of these brothers of mine, you did for me" (Matt. 25:40).

Remember when it seemed "forever" that you got up in the middle of the night to feed or change babies? Or worked with the Cub Scouts? Or went to PTA? Well, it's over now, right? Is there anything you wish you had done differently? Or better? Or more? Don't miss the chance to minister *now* to the elderly needy whom God has put in your path.

People Who Live in Glass Houses . . .

Ruth remembers that as a young mother she sometimes called for *one* of her sons: "Steve, Dave, Scott, Buddy," including the name of the dog as she tried to get it right! She also remembers her own young mother calling her "Olga" (Mom's sister's name) or "Judy" (Ruth's sister's name.) We have all made such slips. As we age we see it more. Each generation sees the older one losing mental acuity. Even *we* sometimes ask the same questions over and over and repeat the same stories. We notice it more in the elderly, but increasingly learn to forgive their lapses, even as we are forgiven for ours.

Both as family counselors and general observers of

humankind, our hearts break when we see sandwich-years persons trying to "set it straight" with their elders or "teach them a lesson."

Stop and ask yourself the effect of telling an aging mother or father or aunt or uncle that you have "already heard that story." When you try to correct them, you are not only being unkind but are doing an unhealthy thing to yourself by ignoring a reality that you need to face and grieve.

Most of us would prefer to deny the fact that our elder loved ones *are* losing their capabilities. By our perfectionistic nagging, we keep alive deep within ourselves the comforting fantasy that life will continue as it was in "the good old days" of our childhood. To boost our sense of security, we cling to the notion that they will forever keep the competence we used to need. We find comfort in our own adult identities even as we mourn the decline of those former giants in our lives who made the good old days so precious.

Our nagging serves no useful purpose. And it violates the fourth part of the cogent Four-Way Test promoted by Rotary International as guidelines for everything we say and do: "Will it be beneficial to all concerned?" Let us enjoy the story or litany as if hearing and participating in it for the first time—for each time may well be the *last* time we get that chance.

Handling Unjust Criticism

When you receive such criticism as, "You never spend enough time with me," examine it and profit from any hidden grains of truth.

Often, because an older person forgets what happened only yesterday, caregivers label their complaints as unwarranted attacks and feel like striking back. Fortunately, there are some ways to respond with a soft answer. Shift your mental gears from trying to win a power struggle. The energy you spend in that futile effort can be diverted to ignoring the barb and directing the conversation to more pleasant topics. Often a big smile and a hug will set the stage for a happier visit. You can use these statements as tools for responding to verbal abuse, even if you consider it unfair. (Later, you can try to decipher the reasoning behind the attack. Perhaps your actions have been misunderstood in the past. If so, you may be able to improve the message *you* are sending.)

To criticisms (like, "The only person you ever care about is yourself"):

1. "I'm sorry you feel that way."
2. "Thank you for telling me."
3. "I'll have to think about that."
4. "You may be right."
5. "Oh." This can be said with so many tones of voice that it can convey any of the following:
   "I see what you mean."
   "I'm so sorry to hear that."
   "I register that you have spoken to me."
   "I understand. Go on."
   "Wow! That's interesting. Please tell me more."

To testy questions (like, "Why can't you be more successful, like your sister?"):

6. "Good question!"
7. "I'm not sure."
8. "I wonder."
9. "I wish I knew."
10. "Beats me!"

To any attack, when the time is right:

11. "I must be a terrible disappointment to you."

These simple responses give you a way to show respect without necessarily capitulating or even defending yourself. They maintain a kind of friendly neutrality. They let people know that you honor them enough to listen to them and consider their points of view. As long as you show respect, you convey dignity to your elders. Here shines the paramount priority in relationships: to show respect for others and for ourselves. The way we treat our elders invites our own children to treat us in the same way. As adults, they still have tape recorders in their heads, as they did when they were much younger. They probably will replay the tapes of our lives over and over again. Let the scenes we have played in the past teach honorable lessons for the future.

Withdrawing Risky Privileges

Grandpa, at age eighty-four, finally began to lose the abilities he had taken for granted long past the time that most people possess them. His family members had to sit down and reach a loving consensus about what limitations to put on him and who should tell him. They selected his favorite granddaughter for the job. She went to him tenderly and said, "Grandpa, because we care for you, we are asking you to no longer get up on the roof to shingle it." To help him save face, she added: "We know that you are skillful and agile, but your eyesight is not quite as good as it used to be." Then she mentioned a few other things the family *requested* him not to do, "because we love you so much."

Another family had to tell Grandma, "We love you and care about what happens to you. Because of that, we are asking you not to drive anymore. We notice that your reaction time is a little slower than it used to be. And we are afraid you might get into an accident." Knowing that this loss of mobility would come as quite a shock to her, two of the family took Grandma out for coffee to present this suggestion. Although they asked for her car keys, they reassured her that they had set up a plan for who would drive her whenever she wished to visit the people and places that brought her pleasure.

This courteous, respectful approach does much more for everyone's peace of mind than does a sudden, angry restriction of an older person's independence. One son, while riding with his mother, became so impatient with her driving that he angrily displaced her from the driver's seat and drove her home. There he pocketed her car keys and proclaimed, "That's the last time you'll *ever* drive." In her hurt she threatened to take taxicabs everywhere she wanted to go, and to bill him for the fares.

Here follow some guidelines for tactfully withdrawing privileges that are placing a loved one at risk:

1. *Plan ahead.* Anticipate when your intervention will be necessary, so you can avoid abrupt, spur-of-the-moment ultimatums.

2. *Express appreciation and understanding.* "You have taken such good care of this house for so long, Mom, and we know it breaks your heart to think of leaving it. But you have fallen twice lately, going up and down the stairs. We are afraid for you, so we want to help you relocate to a new place that's all on one level. Please let us do something for *you* for a change."

3. *Voice your own emotions.* Say, "I am concerned," or "We are afraid," as in the above example. This frames the sacrifice you are about to ask of the elderly person as a considerate gesture toward *you*. His or her thought that "I'm doing this for my children" carries much more dignity than "I'm too old," or "They *made* me do it."

4. *Reassure them about future arrangements.* "We have found a place we want to show you" leaves much less uncertainty than "You've got to get out of here."

An Afterword

As those of us in the sandwich years must increasingly compensate for the fading abilities of our elders, we grieve for the loss of their past strengths. Yet, we can enhance the quality of their remaining years and even prolong their time with us if we maintain a loving attitude of cheerful forbearance. To the extent that we respect *their* personhood and offer our care, we ourselves are strengthened and honored in their eyes and in the eyes of a watching world.

9

The Unexpected Death

Dennis

Despite our best care and our maximum patience, we will all lose our older loved ones eventually. Sometimes death comes slowly and painfully, and we are somewhat prepared. At other times it catches us off guard, as it did when Ruth's father died.

Heart Attack!

One sunny July morning, Ruth's father, Eric Flesvig, kissed his wife good-bye and went to play golf at the Village Links. After teeing off at the second hole, he felt sick and sat down under a tree to rest. Suddenly he slumped unconscious. His partners called for paramedics, who quickly got him to the nearest hospital's intensive-care unit.

Ruth, her mom, brother, and several grandchildren soon heard the bad news and rushed to Eric's side. They had some chance to talk to him, not knowing whether he heard. The family alternated between wondering, "Is this the end?" and cheerfully thinking, "He'll pull out of it. He's recovered from two previous heart attacks."

All day Ruth and her family kept the vigil in the ICU. Dad, hooked up to a variety of monitors and machines, seemed not to sense their presence as he struggled to breathe. His loved ones wondered whether to let him rest alone or sit nearby and talk to him for comfort. If they could predict the future, they might know what to do. If Eric was going to live, they should let him rest to gain strength. If he was going to die, they should be right beside him so he would not be alone at the end.

Undecided, they went in and out of Dad's room, careful not to disturb him. Ruth's mom asked for a blanket to cover him because his room felt cold. Since no one told the family how Eric seemed to be doing medically, they felt helpless and abandoned. They had thought that Eric should get oxygen, since he gasped so hard for breath. Although Eric was actually being closely monitored, no doctor appeared, only nurses who seemed unclear about the patient's condition or were not authorized to give the family updates on his condition. (To an anxious family, hospital personnel may *seem* unconcerned, though that is rarely true.)

The other family members left and Ruth sat with her mother in the waiting room. They debated about whether to go home to sleep but decided to stay.

The End

The clock showed 8:21 P.M. when doctors and nurses suddenly ran by the door to the waiting room. A heart monitor evidently indicated an abrupt change for some patient. Was it Eric? What could this emergency mean? Death?

Shortly thereafter, a doctor came up and said those numbing words: "We did all we could. He passed away."

Ruth's little 110-pound mother stood to her feet. Rising to the occasion, she bravely announced, "We had fifty-two years together." Then, ever so slightly, she slumped against her daughter. In that moment, Ruth suddenly became her mother's caretaker, in place of the faithful husband of over half a century.

Ruth and Mom sat down while the medical people went to prepare Eric so they could see him. A chaplain came and talked to them. They prayed. Then Ruth called her brother and sister.

Ruth and her mother went in to see Dad, and it seemed to them as if he were still alive when they looked at his beloved face.

A nurse came in to ask about donation of organs. Ruth looked at Mom. To her surprise she learned that the Flesvigs had never discussed this matter, even though they had written wills and bought grave plots. Mom simply answered the nurse, "I don't think so," and Ruth sensitively supported her mother's wishes. The nurse next asked what funeral home. Mom chose one in her suburb.

Ruth and her mom sat by Dad's body. He was gone. They touched him and kissed him. Ruth stepped out of the room to let Mom have her last moments alone with Eric, to complete in her own way the wedding vow: "till death do us part." The bride of a half-century lovingly committed her groom to rest in the arms of the Lord.

Ruth remembers feeling like an outsider at this private, intimate moment. She was simply the middle offspring from that long, solid marriage just ended. Mommy and Daddy were the "one-flesh," lovers parted only by the hand of death.

The First Twenty-four Hours Alone

Ruth and her mother walked out of the hospital together. Mom said, "I think we'll just have a small family service for Dad." Ruth answered, "Whatever you wish." Ruth recognized keenly the importance of honoring and implementing Mom's wishes at this time, which affected Mom's life more than anyone else's.

As they drove to Mom's home, Ruth had a strange mixed feeling. The familiar lights of the city said that everything was still the same. And yet everything was forever different. It was the first hour of Ruth's life that Dad did not share. For Mom, this hour closed a very long chapter in her life.

After the two drove back to Mom's apartment, Ruth decided to spend the night. She called me to bring over some personal items. At bedtime, Ruth took the twin bed next to Mom's. She told me that "it still smelled like Daddy." Only hours before, he had climbed out of that bed to greet the day. Now he rested in his final sleep.

The next morning, Ruth and Mom went to the funeral home with the clothing Eric's body would wear in his grave. They chose the same dapper sport coat he wore proudly on their fiftieth wedding anniversary. The funeral director gently asked for information about relatives and such, to put into the newspaper obituary notice. Ruth remembers thinking, offended, "How dare you sit there and earn a living off the death of my father!" Although she did not say this aloud, it reflected her sense of helpless rage at the reality of her father's death.

That feeling compounded when they entered a room displaying several different styles of caskets. Ruth recoiled at having to make a commercial decision at this emotional time, but Mom chose a medium-priced casket. Ruth felt it did not matter much, since the device would go into the ground. Out of respect for Eric's dignity, it should not be too cheap. But, out of respect for his thrifty character, it surely should not be the most expensive.

Late that day, a little family conclave gathered around the dining-room table in Mom's apartment. I joined Ruth, her mom, her brother, Bob, who lived nearby, and her sister, Judy, who flew in from Colorado. Our youngest son, Scott, also was with us.

Ruth says she experienced a kind of déjà vu around that table. She had sat with loved ones, including her grandmother, when Grandpa died thirty-three years earlier.

Now she saw her mother sitting at the table, pushing food around on her plate with a fork and saying, "I'm not very hungry." In that moment, Ruth remembered her newly widowed grandma doing the very same thing.

Honoring the Deceased

Eric's loved ones assembled at a room in the funeral home to honor the life of this fine man. This particular funeral service included only the immediate family: Ruth and myself, her mother and sister and brother, and several grandchildren.

The gathered family members simply sat in a circle around the casket, sharing their precious memories about Eric Flesvig. They had wisely allowed plenty of time for this leisurely reminiscing. Sometime later that morning, the hearse and its procession of two or three cars left for the cemetery. Only the immediate family ever viewed Eric's body in the casket.

At the graveside the family held a simple commitment service. I read some words from Scripture. Then we all sang a hymn that Grandpa loved: "How Great Thou Art!" The unique role of celebrant enabled me to bond to my mother-in-law more closely than ever before.

Months later, Ruth's brother arranged to have a white pine tree planted adjoining the second hole of the golf course where his father had collapsed. He and Ruth and Mom went to look at it and to read the plaque honoring Eric Flesvig. As they turned to leave, Mom commented, "I'm always walking away." She remembered walking away from Dad after he died, after seeing him in the funeral home, after leaving his coffin at the grave. Now she walked away from the tree that would live on after him.

A Celebration of Life

Several days after Grandpa's burial, the family put on a celebration of the life of Eric Flesvig and "invited" their friends by announcing the time and place of the service in a newspaper notice. The family used the sanctuary of the church that the Flesvigs had attended. Instead of displaying the body in a casket, as occurs at many such services, the family placed an excellent photograph of Eric right at the entry to the sanctuary.

One of the grandsons opened the service with a prayer. Another read a Scripture passage. In planning the service, the family made sure that any member who wanted to play a part could do so. They gave first priority to the wishes of the most bereaved, the widow, regarding what to feature.

Ruth says that if we had this memorial to do over again, we might do a few things differently. We might not arrange for a pastor to come and preach a short message. Although he did an excellent job at Eric's memorial service, we already had a full-enough agenda with adequately gifted family members. We would also probably prepare and distribute a small printed program of the service as a remembrance.

(In the case of my own mother, we conducted a memorial service three weeks after her death. This arrangement spares the bereaved the added pressure of having to schedule a ceremony within a few days of the death.)

If the deceased has expressed any wishes concerning how to honor his or her passing, place a priority on fulfilling those desires. We heard of one funeral in which someone played the Penn State Fight Song as the pallbearers carried the casket out to the hearse. Probably some loved one remembered this lively, spirited man once exclaiming years earlier "Boy, when I go I'd like to have them play our Fight Song!" Such observances say something about a person's identity, what he or she cared about, and the impact the deceased wanted to make on others.

Informing Loved Ones

The day of Dad Flesvig's death found one of our sons overseas on a study trip. We phoned him and agreed that he need not make a special trip home but should continue his trip as planned.

Another of our college age sons was leading a group of junior high boys on a wilderness camping expedition. We telephoned to the base camp and asked them to bring our son in to a telephone to call us about urgent family news. We debated about having the messenger tell him, "Your grandfather died," and decided that he should hear such solemn news only from the lips of a family member and not a stranger.

We were wrong! In the hours it took our son to get to a phone, he suffered great anguish from not knowing *what* catastrophe had befallen the family. He told us he felt awkward about breathing a sigh of relief over the phone when he learned it was "only" Grandpa who had died, since he had feared that it might be his dear brother traveling overseas. Although Eric Flesvig died suddenly, he died in the fullness of time. If we had it to do again, we would have the messenger tell our son the exact reason for the extraordinary call.

Generally, when informing someone of the death of a loved one, we preface the news with something like: "I'm afraid that I have some sad news to report." In that moment the listener prepares emotionally to receive the shock. If a particular family member has slipped toward death for some days, the listener naturally braces to hear *that* ailing one's name. However, with sudden, unexpected deaths, listeners often prepare to hear even worse news than we have to tell them.

Bonding with Survivors

After the moving memorial service for Grandpa Flesvig, we regretted that we had not worked harder at gathering *all* the family members that reasonably could come. At the time, it seemed inconvenient for some of them to take time away from their activities and travel the distance to attend the service. In retrospect, we think we all missed an unrepeatable occasion to bind ourselves a bit closer to each other. So, we urge this motto: say "Yes" to such an opportunity unless you have an extraordinary reason for saying "No."

With any who decide not to attend, do not make them feel guilty. Include them in the spirit of the event. Send them a tape recording of the ceremony. Tell them what happened and how you all felt, in as much detail as they can appreciate. Convey the idea that "I felt as close to you as if you had been right there at my side." Let the loss of a loved one link the living family and friends closer together than ever.

At a time of death, relatives and friends express their compassion by bringing food. It gives them a gracious and practical way to show their love and sympathy. Let those who want to eat do so; excuse others who do not wish to partake. Don't make a big deal of it.

An Afterword

The day after Eric died, Ruth noticed on her mother's dresser a familiar little book whose binding no longer held the pages together. Ruth opened it and glanced at a few portions. The book told a story about the marriage of Eric and Ruth Flesvig—their wedding and how they celebrated each of their fifty-two anniversaries. Ruth's mom had added a final entry when she recorded the death of her beloved partner.

Ruth pondered the deeper meaning of that book. She saw it as a book of love, a book of life, a book of death. Although the binding didn't last, the pages—aged, fragile, wet with tears—stood as a timeless parable of the godly woman widowed one July evening.

10

The Man with Nine Lives

Ruth

Not all older-generation deaths are as unexpected as Eric Flesvig's. In the case of Dennis's dad, Murray Gibson, there was a period of hospitalization and off-again/on-again remissions that somewhat prepared us for the final ending of his life.

"He Won't Last Long"

The eastbound traffic in our lane on Roosevelt Road was stalled at the green light. Dennis got out to help the driver of a pickup truck in front of us replace the load of angle iron that had slid off onto the pavement. Dennis commented on how weird it seemed to be doing such an ordinary, tedious thing at such an unusual moment in his life. We were traveling to the hospital, anticipating his father's deathbed scene. We wondered if we would have a chance to see him before his last breath. Twenty minutes earlier, Dad's cardiologist had called urgently to say, "You'd better come quickly. This looks like the end. I don't think he'll last much longer."

We arrived at the hospital and went somberly up the elevator to Murray's floor. To our surprise the staff greeted us cheerfully. Murray himself received us with his characteristically spry, "Hello there!" To everyone's surprise, he had rallied—once again. The cardiologist shook his head and quipped, "The man has nine lives!"

False Alarms

On November 5, 1984, Murray Gibson, age seventy-six, had called an ambulance to take him to the hospital because of chest pain and difficulty breathing. The diagnosis was congestive heart failure, with some emphysema. Dennis's father had paid a similar visit to this hospital a few weeks earlier, staying just overnight.

This time the doctors kept Murray longer, for tests and observation. During this time his condition worsened; he nearly died twice in the first couple of weeks. Then he settled into a frustrating routine. The medical personnel needed to stabilize one system in his body before they could work on the next. One treatment mode hinged on another's success.

This patient had smoked cigarettes continuously for fifty years. He had quit "cold turkey" a few years earlier, after heart-bypass surgery. In recent weeks he had started smoking again out of boredom.

Three or four times, the hospital called us to come quickly because the end seemed near. Murray rallied each time. On one of those grim occasions, Dennis assembled all three of his brothers from out of state. He summoned them with the message that this was certainly the last time they would see their father alive, if indeed he survived long enough for them to arrive. Their visit turned out to invigorate Murray into an alert state

in which he breathed well, joked, and seemed entirely
like his old self.

Dennis felt foolish for having called his brothers
together for this false alarm. Instead of a time of mourning, the day had turned into one of joviality. Nobody
talked about death, nobody said good-bye openly, nobody
shed tears. The next day, after his sons left, Murray
returned to his labored breathing and blurred thinking.
He remembered little of the visit.

The End Comes

The hospital had a utilization-review policy. That
meant they had to discharge Medicare patients when
medical personnel could no longer justify keeping them
for care offered elsewhere. Dennis did some research
about nursing-care facilities in the area. He found a new
one near our home, eager to fill its quota, and offering
financial incentives. We read literature about the place,
visited it, liked the personnel, and presented a sales pitch
to Murray about it. After voicing some resistance, he
finally agreed to move from the hospital to this new facility on December 12. We would pick him up in our car
and make this transfer. Once Murray made up his mind
to it, he seemed eager to proceed.

We took a day off from work to get Murray moved and
well settled into his new quarters. First we went to the
apartment building where he had been living and picked
up his mail, telling the people there the good news that
Murray had recovered so well that he would graduate
from the hospital that day. Then we drove to the hospital and took the elevator up to Murray's floor. We
expected an especially bright greeting from the cheerful
faces of the nurses and aides who had become so dear to
us in recent weeks.

This time, however, as we got off the elevator, they
took one look at us and turned their eyes away. One ran

to get the cardiologist, who took us into a conference room and began a slow speech: "We were getting all of your father's belongings together. He was dressed to leave, in high spirits and eager for your visit, and apparently went into the bathroom and . . . ."

At this point Dennis thought, "Oh, no. He's fallen and broken his hip and now has to stay in the hospital and mend from *that.*" I had a different intuition, since I looked at the doctor and asked, "Is he dead?" The doctor quietly answered, "Yes."

Dennis's immediate reaction included disbelief, sadness, relief, and guilt for feeling relief. He almost laughed at the irony of the timing. He heaved a big sigh because an ordeal had ended. On the other hand, Murray's life was over and his son could not complete the mission he had begun. Dennis had wanted to honor his father by taking him to that new nursing home. Now he would not have the chance. All that research counted for nothing now. Of course, now we would not have to go through that move and all the caution to make sure everything went right. We no longer faced obligatory visits to a dying man. We no longer waited on pins and needles for the call to come that he had died. But the irony of it! As he was leaving the hospital, the man with nine lives suddenly had need of a tenth.

The Finality of Death

For five or ten minutes we talked with the doctor while nurses prepared Dad's body in his bed for us to see him. We entered the room reverently and tearfully, cried, then mentioned how calm and peaceful he looked. We sat down beside him and took his hands, which still felt warm and limp. As we took our time with him there for about half an hour, his flesh gradually became cooler and stiffer.

Since Murray seemed just asleep, Dennis needed to know if he was really dead. He tried to waken Dad, just to see up close this obstinate phenomenon of death. He took his father's hand, shook it, and called, "Dad, it's me, Den. Wake up! Talk to me!" Not a budge. Then Dennis tried the ultimate test: "Dad, I have a joke for you. Hey, did you hear the one about . . .?" Not a ripple arose from the dead man. Murray had always relished a joke. Nothing animated him more than the statement, "I got a joke for you." Anyone knowing him would have said that those words would rouse him from *anything*. They didn't. We saw the stubborn finality of death.

We lingered for a while, reminiscing about "beef kow," talking mostly to each other but occasionally to Murray. We interspersed our informal sentences of prayer with thanks for Murray, perspectives on life and death and eternity, and wonderment at God's greatness compared with our fragile brevity.

While at his dad's bedside, Dennis picked up the phone and dialed his mother. He announced to her that Dad had just died. She matter-of-factly said, "Oh." Dennis told her that he was right there, with the phone just inches from Dad's face. Even then Dennis tried to build a bridge between his long-alienated parents: "Well, I think he still loved you, Mom. If he could have had the chance a few minutes ago, I believe he would have said, 'Good-bye, Marguerite. I'm going now. Take care, you hear? I love you.' " She cried for a few seconds, then said, as if to Murray, "Well, I loved you, too. You were once my sun, moon, and stars. Good-bye to you." Then Dennis asked if she wanted to come and see Dad one last time. She said, "No, this was enough."

Final Arrangements

Dennis's parents had arranged some years before to donate their bodies to science through the Demonstrators organization in Chicago. (Medical students use bodies thus donated to help them learn human anatomy.) The family therefore faced no costs for burial or cremation.

Weeks earlier, Dennis had already signed all the papers necessary to have a local funeral home transport Dad's remains to Demonstrators. The morticians were also to arrange for obituaries to appear in newspapers that Dennis specified. Later, they would make sure that he received certified copies of the death certificate that he could use as executor of Murray's will to gain access to bank accounts and other records.

From Murray's deathbed, Dennis telephoned one of his brothers, who spread the word to the other two. He simply told the story of Murray's last hour and our final good-byes on their behalf. The sons did not gather in memoriam. They felt they had adequately said their good-byes weeks earlier on the "false alarm" visit.

None of the four sons had ever felt particularly close to the father who had skipped in and out of their lives. Murray had been a manic-depressive who drank too much and created periodic havoc, repeatedly breaking the heart and hopes of their beloved mother. Dennis captured his main sense of loss with the words, "I wish things could have been different." Then he called the funeral parlor and they took over from there. We took one last look at Murray, said one last farewell, and walked out of his hospital room, never to see his face again.

In the days that followed, only one or two people called to offer condolences. We held no wake, no funeral or memorial service for Murray, who had few living friends.

The Hospital Staff

We said appreciative good-byes to all the fine staff persons with whom we had become friends in this saga of life and death. Tears filled each one's eyes. They had grown to love Murray, too, and our sorrow compounded theirs. We suddenly realized that they go through this kind of attachment and loss day in and day out. How frustrating to have brought a man back from the brink of death, prepared him for departure, and then have him die before their eyes. If we were in their shoes we would have felt defeated, especially because we had applied our best medical skills, thought we had triumphed, then saw it all turn to ashes. We left with a fresh awareness of the courage and resiliency it takes for caregivers who work with dying people.

Disposing of Belongings

We went back to Dad's apartment building, which we had left about an hour earlier. We walked in and said, "Change of plans. Murray will not be moving to a new place. He died just before we arrived." The women to whom we announced this flinched in disbelief. Tears came to their eyes, and one sighed, "Isn't that a shame!" It was gratifying to learn that others would miss him, too.

We asked for the key to Murray's room, thinking we might just look it over and remove a few things. When we got there we realized that we had an entire unscheduled day ahead of us. We looked at each other and said, "Want to clean up the whole place?" Dennis's mom did not want any of it, so we rolled up our sleeves and dug into all Murray's remaining earthly possessions.

We threw away about one-third of it. The remainder we loaded into our Chevy Suburban and hauled home. The process gave us plenty of chances for farewell reveries, punctuated by occasional tears. We packed Murray's clothing to launder and donate to the needy through the Repeat Boutique. Later, his boxes and drawers of papers took us weeks to sort. Dennis, as executor of Dad's will, had to search for a number of papers clarifying details about where he could find a particular bank account or retirement fund or insurance policy.

What an odd experience it was to clean out a man's entire belongings in a few hours. It took such a short time to handle residue from seventy-six years of living. I eventually made up a book of poems Murray had written and duplicated a copy for each of his sons as a Christmas gift titled, "The Best of Murray Gibson."

How Not to Do It

We have heard of an old-fashioned tradition that horrifies us. Sometimes, after loved ones go to the funeral of a family member, they return home to find all the departed one's belongings removed. Some well-meaning friends—often without authorization—take on this removal task, as if it does the survivors a great favor. For example, a widow might return home from burying her husband and see little there to remind her of him. His closet stands empty. His dresser drawers contain nothing. Mere indentations remain where his favorite chair sat. What an additional shock to her, even if she had agreed to have it done. The man and everything having to do with him suddenly disappear from her life as if they never existed.

We consider this practice unwise. It should *never* be done without the permission of the immediate survivor(s). Even then, the bereaved should be discouraged from making such a hasty decision in the immediate aftermath of a death. It deprives them of a valuable way to work through their grief. They need a chance to pore over the belongings of their beloved, one piece at a time, saying a little bit more of their "Good-bye" as they dispose of each item in their own time and way.

Those household items belong to these wounded people, who need to have their familiar environment remain stable while they gradually recover from the shock of their loss. Later on, friends might make themselves *available* to help survivors clear out these belongings, but let them not intrude. And they should be wary of participating in this process until they are convinced that the bereaved are thinking clearly.

How to Be Helpful

As a friend, relative, or pastor, if the immediate survivors seem so disabled by their loss that they don't get on with their lives after a reasonable period of time, you can offer some helpful nudges. Think primarily in terms of connecting them with the mainstream of life—moving them on into the future, rather than amputating them from their past.

If asked to help survivors go through the belongings and mark items for certain persons, be unobtrusive. As a relative or close friend, you may remember some conversation to the effect that the deceased wanted such-and-such a picture or chair or vase to go to so-and-so. Share this information if the bereaved seem to welcome it. (In the absence of prearrangements, people who want certain items often simply say, "I would particularly like to have this chair and these two pictures. Do any of you have a problem with that?" Not all families communicate in such cooperative, uncomplicated language, but we recommend this approach.) "Outsiders," no matter how closely they have been attached to the deceased or the immediate family should be tactful about offering suggestions and sensitive to the often-ambivalent emotions at play among those directly involved in the mourning process.

An Afterword

When we returned home from cleaning out Murray's apartment, we checked our answering service for messages. Among several, one brief one jabbed us with still another irony. It said, "Call your dad." The phone call had come about five minutes after we had left home to get him. Murray had still been alive then and had some word for Dennis that he never got to hear.

11

The Lingering Death

Ruth

Perhaps the most devastating words we can hear a doctor say about a loved one are "I'm sorry—it's cancer." Somehow that translates immediately in one's mind as "death sentence," and it often is. For, despite the great strides being made by medical researchers and the encouragement and hope to be found in remission statistics, the fact remains that many of our elders will die a lingering death from this disease, as did Dennis's wonderful mother, Marguerite Gibson. If you are facing this painful ordeal in your own family, we can but hope that you will learn as much about faith and courage from the cancer victim as we did a few years ago.

Two Moons with Mom

Dennis's high school friends always found a warm welcome in his home from his vibrant mother. These friends gradually evolved an affectionate nickname for her. They called her by just the first syllable of the word *Mother* and spelled it "Muth." She fondly adopted the name and used it to her dying day.

During his senior year of high school, Dennis built a small telescope as part of a physics project. Late one night he finished it and pointed it at the full moon. To his delight he saw craters and mountains in crisp detail. Excitedly he went into the house and awakened Muth to invite her outside at one o'clock in the morning to see the moon through his telescope. Despite having her sleep interrupted, she cheerfully put on a robe and went into the backyard. She looked through the eyepiece and exclaimed and marveled over the sight, sharing in her son's thrill over his achievement and what it enabled them to see together that moonlit night.

In reminiscing during the weeks before her death, Dennis and his mother were to recall that moonlit night and relive the happiness of sharing its experience. Then, two hours after she died on the night of December 5, 1987, Dennis walked alone around our block. Once again there was a full moon. He looked up at it and said to himself, "The moon once again marks my connection to my mother. I will always remember her whenever I gaze up at a full moon."

"It's Cancer"

Symptoms and diagnosis

Twelve months before she died of ovarian cancer at age 76, Muth complained of abdominal pain. For that month of December, she tried to handle the symptoms by controlling her diet. In January she went to a hospital for tests as an outpatient. The diagnosis came back as probable cancer of the ovaries, with possible involvement of the large intestine. Recommendation: hysterectomy and surgical removal of some of the large intestine (possibly necessitating a colostomy), followed by chemotherapy. Chances of surviving as long as five years after this treatment were about 30 percent.

To Be or Not to Be

For weeks, Marguerite debated about whether or not to have the surgery. At the age of twenty-three she had watched her father die of colon cancer. She remembered having hated the smell that filled the house as he got sicker day after day. Muth had vowed that she would never put her loved ones through a similar ordeal. So, for the month of February, she read about cancer. She tried more herbs and dietary remedies but also took a course on death-and-dying at a local senior center.

Dennis's mother asked friends and loved ones their advice about whether to go ahead with the expensive and painful surgery. One after another said, "Of course, it is up to you, but I think you should go for it." Most expressed the thought that except for the cancer, she was in good health, "young" for her age, and thus stood a great chance of being in that small percent of survivors. Furthermore, many believed she would have a story to tell others that would help them make the difficult decision that now faced her.

Pain finally made the decision for her. Her particular form of tumor grew rapidly. Her abdomen swelled so that she looked pregnant. It hurt. If euthanasia had been available, she might have seriously considered it. She decided instead to take her best chance for survival by having the surgery.

Living Wills and Colostomies

Before going into surgery, Marguerite signed a "living will" that she had picked up from her course on death-and-dying. In it she specified that no extraordinary measures be used to prolong her life in the event she neared death during surgery. She wanted no life-support systems, no pushing on her chest to restart a failed heart. In her mind this also meant "no colostomy."

Note: State laws differ on the legal status of a living will and on the recommended wording. In any event, it is an option to be considered by anyone who wishes to document his wishes for family and medical authorities. (See also "legal arrangements," in chapter 12, especially the reference to Durable Power of Attorney.)

On March 13, 1987, Marguerite underwent the surgery. The surgeon later explained that he had to remove several feet of the large intestine. He said he could not just reconnect the severed ends because they would leak fluids out of the seam into Muth's body cavity, causing a slow, agonizing death from infection. Medical ethics called for him to perform a colostomy to complete the surgery.

When Marguerite awoke from her surgery and discovered she had had a colostomy, she felt betrayed. She felt consigned against her will to violate her vow not to have the same type of death as her father's. When she finally understood the surgeon's dilemma, she accepted the necessity for the dreaded colostomy. To her credit, soon after leaving the hospital, Muth dicovered an ostomy support group and later devoted herself to helping others whom she considered less fortunate than herself.

Just before leaving the hospital to live in our home, Muth got some lessons from a colostomy nurse. What a relief to find the nurse to be a cheerful young woman whose competence and bright smile went miles to reassure Muth that her colostomy was no horrible stigma that would make her an outcast from polite society. We sat in on these lessons so that we could learn how to change the appliance in the event that Marguerite's shaking hands might prevent her.

The colostomy rerouted Muth's intestine to a hole in her left side, just below the level of her navel. She could no longer have normal bowel movements, and her intestines would periodically empty their contents into a plastic bag fitted to a small protrusion of intestine through her side. Someone would need to empty and clean the colostomy bag once a day or so. Every few days, someone would have to replace the old bag with a new one and clean around the protrusion to prevent infection.

At one moment during this hygiene training, the worst imaginable to Muth's mind happened. A bubble of gas emerged from her exposed intestinal protrusion and made a sound. That wonderful nurse immediately made light of the incident by joking, "Oh, it's talking to us!" It relieved the tension considerably. Nevertheless, Muth looked at Dennis and asked in almost a panic, "Are you turned off?" Dennis answered gently, "Mom, you took care of me when I could not take care of myself. Now I consider it a privilege to learn how to take care of you when you need me to."

A Cheerful Patient

Muth never wanted to burden anyone with her problems. If she could have mustered enough strength to resume the daily routine she followed before surgery, she would have. But, because of her weakened condition, we insisted that she come to live with us. We had a spare bedroom that she could consider her new studio apartment. Seeing no better option, she reluctantly agreed.

As we look back on those days, we recognize that Muth made a lovely inner decision that she lived out fully to the last moment of her life, nine months later. She set herself to avoid inconveniencing anyone else with her illness and *chose* to remain cheerful, always asking others about themselves instead of focusing on her condition. Muth actually ministered to those who were her caregivers in her last days.

Muth lived in our home after she left the hospital in March 1987 until she died in our arms on December 5. Until about September, she maintained an active life. She cooked, did correspondence, and talked on the phone as much as a teenager. She especially enjoyed the freedom of driving her car around to visit friends and former patients for whom she had cared as a practical nurse. Although she usually stayed in bed until we left for work in the morning, sometimes we would return a few min-

utes later, to get something we had forgotten. Then we
would find the radio blaring happy music with Muth up
and singing, having the place to herself.

Every week or two, Debbie, the visiting nurse, came to
check Mom's condition and review her colostomy care.
Each time at the door, Debbie would stop, shake her head,
and say to me alone, "She's such a neat lady, but she won't
live long."

Muth came to hear us at nearly every seminar and
Sunday school class we taught. She joined us for a play at
a dinner theater to celebrate my birthday. Every week she
sat in the audience during broadcasts of our hour-long
cable TV show, "Positive Living" and told us it made her
feel like a celebrity. She often spoke from the audience as
I came around with a roving microphone in the second
half-hour of the show.

In late September, a day came when Dennis's mom felt
too tired to come to our show. A few days later she went
out with us to a restaurant. She nibbled at a piece of car-
rot cake, but could not finish it. We now look back on
that as the last time she set foot outside our house.

Some Words About Chemotherapy

Months earlier, the surgeon had said he got 95 percent
of the cancerous tissue. The rest would require follow-up
chemotherapy. He explained that it would cause nausea
and make her hair fall out. Without chemotherapy, he
said, the tumor would probably grow back rapidly.
Within months Muth would again have the painful,
swollen abdomen that prompted her surgery in the first
place. However, a second surgery like the first would
then no longer be an option.

Muth hated nausea and said at the time that she would
rather die than go through the rigors of chemotherapy.
Following her surgery she felt better than she had for
months. Not wanting to disturb that feeling of well-being,
she grabbed on to the shreds of uncertainty in the doc-

tor's statement that the tumor would *probably* grow back. That meant it *might not,* even without chemotherapy.

We convinced Muth to get a second medical opinion rather than delay chemotherapy if it might save her life. I took her to a woman oncologist recommended by the local cancer society, thinking that a woman doctor would be more gentle and understanding toward this condition in a "sister's" body.

After examining Muth and reviewing her medical records, this oncologist strongly recommended aggressive chemotherapy. She spoke about the grim side effects of chemotherapy in even more graphic and harsh terms than the surgeon had. It sounded so obnoxious to Muth that she decided she would rather live only a few months without nausea than to *possibly* prolong her life with such high discomfort.

Not knowing any better, we supported Mom's choice, but a few months later we learned about another oncologist from our trusted family physician. He said of this oncologist, "He's a *real* doctor. He'll make house calls." When Muth began to complain about weakness, nausea, and a growing fullness in her abdomen, Dennis took her to this new oncologist. Dennis wanted to protect his mother from the kind of insensitivity that I felt the female oncologist had inflicted on her.

This new man turned out to have a gentle, reassuring bedside manner. He explained that he had discovered he could regulate the dosage and timing of chemotherapy so that many of his patients did not experience adverse side effects. He implied that the chances for a cure from chemotherapy would have been much higher if Muth had begun it within a few weeks of her surgery. Now, about four months later, he offered only a slim chance. He could definitely say, however, that without it she would have *no* chance of slowing the tumor's malignant growth.

With our encouragement Muth decided to give this new doctor's chemotherapy a try. To her delight she had no side effects. She had always loved shrimp cocktails but recently had lost her appetite to the point where she quipped, "I can't look a shrimp in the face." In answer, the oncologist told her, "Marguerite, that's what the chemotherapy is for—to arrest that growth so that you can regain your appetite."

His prophecy proved correct. During July and August, Muth had eight chemotherapy treatments without nausea or hair loss. She regained her appetite and felt stronger. For a while, the tumor did not grow any larger, so we all thought, "Hey, it's working. We did not wait too long after all."

Hospice

Our hopes were dashed when the tumor started growing again and the symptoms returned. Chemotherapy would no longer work. The doctor discontinued it, also explaining that radiation therapy would not work for her kind of cancer. Finally, he introduced us to some new vocabulary terms: "terminal care," and "hospice."

The Concept

Traditionally, the word *hospice* has meant any shelter for travelers or the disadvantaged. Often in the past, monastic orders have maintained hospices. More recently, "hospice" has come to mean a program that helps terminal patients die as painlessly as possible either at home or in a special wing of a hospital. Although hospice personnel offer services to the dying patient as necessary, they prefer to teach and encourage family members to provide the needed care. Hospice patients are most often dying of cancer, but other disabling conditions are also the focus of their services.

Of several hospice programs available in our area, Muth chose one approved by Medicare. This meant that necessary items such as a hospital-type bed, oxygen, a commode, and prescription medications did not cost

Muth or the family anything. By covering the cost of such items at home, Medicare saves the far-greater cost of terminal care in hospitals. We would like to see much more extensive funding and encouragement of hospice programs by Medicare (and other health-insurance programs) as a way to reduce the drain on our nation's social security system and on an individual's financial assets.

Hospice programs rarely charge patients or their families for their services. They rely heavily on volunteers to provide most of the emotional support for patients and family members. Funds for the few professional and administrative staff persons usually come from private donations or community funds such as United Way.

What Hospice Did for Us

Deloris was a hospice employee who came about once a week to give Muth a bed bath. She became like family to us for the last two months of Muth's life. As they chatted, the conversation supplied even more benefit than the physical care. Muth would tell Deloris things that she would not mention to us for fear of burdening us, though Deloris selectively passed some of these matters on to us to help us better understand the patient. For example, Muth worried that we walked around the house much too quietly in an effort not to disturb her. She felt better when we started banging things around a little more to create the sounds of a normal bustling household!

Deloris and the other splendid hospice workers we met did their tasks as acts of worship. They took to heart the admonition of Jesus: "I was sick and you looked after me. . . . whatever you did for one of the least of these brothers of mine, you did for me" (Matt. 25:36, 40). Jesus laid this down as a mark of those who will enter eternal life with him.

We were asked for well-worn, soft, thin towels with which to dry Muth. Deloris said that they work better than the big, fluffy new towels that don't bend and flex with the thin bodies of the dying. Such little nuances of expertise symbolized for us the cups of cold water that Jesus instructed people to offer, just as he would (Matt. 10:42).

As the disease progressed, a total of eighteen persons sat with Muth for hours at a time while we were off to work, during the last six weeks when she no longer left her bed. This cadre of helpers included neighbors, family members, church friends, Marguerite's best childhood girl friend, and at least seven hospice volunteers who were otherwise complete strangers to us. Dennis's brothers were able to visit only occasionally because they lived so far away. One church friend, a nurse, taught Dennis how to give injections of painkilling and anti-nausea medications. Muth needed these for her last two weeks. She joked that she always knew Dennis would someday be a "real doctor" who could give shots.

We learned several timeless lessons from the good hospice people and the others who so lovingly cared for Muth. Perhaps the most important one is that only when we come to grips with our own mortality do we know life and how to live it. When we tend the dying, we know that we, too, will surely die. A home privileged to house the dying knows the wonder and miracle of both life and death.

Mom's Dream of Dad

Between one and two months before she died, Muth started most days with a pleasant good-morning conversation with Dennis. One morning when he went in to greet her he found her positively radiant. She told him the following dream, which had deeply affected her that night:

> I dreamed I was walking in heaven. Everything was just peaceful and fragrant and lovely. The first person who came up to me was Murray. As he approached me, he

looked so clean and friendly. He came up to me with his arms wide open, smiled, and said, "Everything's okay now."

"That says it all," she concluded. "Everything *is* okay now between him and me." With that dream, Marguerite had taken a significant step of forgiveness and relief. She had found Murray to be the greatest source of pain in her entire life. The only way she had known to protect herself against his harshness was to harden herself and not even have eye contact with him. Fortunately, this dream and her acceptance of it allowed her to put to rest a bitter chapter in her life before she died.

Gathering the Clan

That fall the whole Gibson family gathered at our house for an unforgettable celebration of Thanksgiving Day—and of the life of Marguerite Gibson. She could then barely talk and went in and out of consciousness as Methadone painkiller injections took effect. Family members each had an individual opportunity to say good-bye to Muth. Mostly we affirmed each other as part of a loving family.

As a novel highlight for this Thanksgiving occasion, we scheduled a surprise event. We had everyone go downstairs until we signaled them to come to the living room. There we had spread out fifteen orange T-shirts we had specially imprinted in dark brown weeks before: "Gibson Family Classic, Thanksgiving, 1987." The "classic" meant a run outdoors around the block. Afterward we all convened in Muth's bedroom where she greeted us by waving her own orange T-shirt up and down. We know she would have said, "Yay!" if she'd had the strength.

The Sunday after Thanksgiving we all assembled around Mom's bed just before the out-of-towners left. We spoke our appreciation for her and the family she had headed and we concluded by singing together the chorus: "Alleluia." On the last time through, we improvised the words, "How we love you, how we love you. . . ." This was deep, heartfelt grieving.

The End Comes

All during Saturday, December 5, we thought it might be the last day of Mom's life. Her breathing had become more difficult; her energy had sapped more and more. As evening approached, we made her as comfortable as we could. Then we went downstairs to watch a rented video-tape: *A Trip to Bountiful.* The heroine of this charming story is an elderly woman living with her son and his wife in the city. One day she boldly takes off on a bus trip to her tiny hometown of Bountiful, Texas. Several times during this tender movie, one hears this hymn:

> Softly and tenderly, Jesus is calling,
> Calling for you and for me;
> See, on the portals he's waiting and watching,
> Watching for you and for me.
> Come home, come home,
> Ye who are weary, come home;
> Earnestly, tenderly, Jesus is calling,
> Calling, O sinner, come home!

How fitting that hymn was to the mood of that special Saturday.

Muth's Last Breath

About eight that evening, I said to Dennis, "Let's go upstairs and check Muth." We turned off the video player, went upstairs, and poked our heads into Muth's room. She reclined in a half-sitting position, moaning slightly and tossing her head from side to side. As we entered, she startled a bit, caught her breath, and began choking because she simply did not have enough energy to clear her lungs. We lifted her full upright and helped her try to catch her breath. She made a few feeble attempts to cough but just could not.

Dennis recognized that she was losing consciousness. He looked across his mother's bed into my eyes and said, "Honey, this is it." Then he bent down, put his cheek against Mom's and said, "I love you, Mom. You've been a good mother. Thank you. Good-bye." Then he prayed, "Father, receive your daughter Marguerite into your waiting arms."

There was no Grim Reaper—just a gentle, quiet, natural transition. We had a sense of a small cordial committee of angels having come into the room to escort her. We simply sat with her, each holding one of her hands, watching as her eyes dimmed. We saw the contractions of her mouth become less and less frequent. The carotid artery in her neck gradually beat more slowly and weakly until, after about ten minutes, we saw no more pulse.

Phone Calls

Dennis called the funeral home with which he had made arrangements weeks earlier. Then he called each of his brothers. He began by saying, "This is the call you've been wondering about." He told them the story of Mom's last day and final minutes.

Soon after hanging up from the last call, Dennis answered the doorbell for the morticians, who had backed an unmarked Chevy Suburban into our driveway, near the front door. They brought upstairs a two-wheeled dolly fitted with a blanket and two sturdy belts. After asking us to leave the room, they strapped Muth's body to the dolly and wheeled it out. At this point, the phone rang. I answered it and spent the next ten minutes with a well-wisher who extolled Muth's life. When I hung up, the body and the Suburban had already disappeared. If Dennis and I had it to do again, we would have let the phone go unanswered. During those unrepeatable moments, we would have wanted to stand arm-in-arm, sobbing as we saw the last ever of Muth.

A Son's Feelings

Dennis had watched alone as the men bumped the blanketed body down the stairs. They apparently did their job well, sensitively and reverently. But he told me later that they seemed like butchers to him, hauling a mere heavy weight of meat down the stairs. That person who had been "Muth" was now just an object to be moved around with industrial equipment.

I learned that in the midst of his mixed resentment and sorrow, Dennis felt almost a comic pity for the poor guy who came as assistant to the mortician. Although the young man stood outside Mom's bedroom with the dolly, trying to keep his face as unexpressive as possible, he could not win in a situation like this. Probably the assistant believed that if he looked friendly, Dennis would have thought, "What are you grinning about? Don't you know my mother just died?" If he looked sad, Dennis might have thought, "What are *you* looking so gloomy about? She wasn't *your* mother."

After the morticians left, Dennis took that walk around the block, alone, under the full moon of his mother's final day on earth.

In Memoriam

In her desire not to burden anybody, Muth had told us that she did not want any formal ceremony after her death. She asked simply that we fly all family members out to Santa Barbara the following May, using some of the money we would inherit from her to buy the tickets. There, on the day before her seventy-seventh birthday, she wanted us to "invade the beach and have fun with each other." Then we could honor her by remembering that she had looked forward to her loved ones basking in the sun together.

We carried out her second wish but modified the first. Since she did not want to inconvenience us with a traditional service we called it a "Celebration of the Life of

Marguerite Gibson." We considered it not a burden but a privilege because we realized that many people loved her and wished to have some way to celebrate what her life had meant to them. So we arranged a service at a church she had attended during her years at "605." It was conveniently scheduled on Saturday, the day after Christmas, three weeks after Mom's death.

We had predicted that as many as forty people might come. But when over a hundred crowded into that chapel, we knew we had done the right thing for these friends and for our own sense of closure.

Dennis opened by briefly telling who Marguerite Gibson was. He shared some personal memories that characterized her goodness. Then he showed part of a videotape from one of our TV shows on which Muth had spoken. The subject of that show was "The Importance of Dad." In it Muth told of a time when she was about four years old and her father rocked her in a rocking chair while he sang "In the Sweet By and By." At the conclusion of Mom's two-minute story, Dennis clicked off the video player and turned on an audio recording of George Beverly Shea singing "In the Sweet By and By."

The video helped everyone there to experience Marguerite as they had known her in life—vibrant, pleasant, youthful, articulate. We would recommend such a feature for any memorial celebration whenever possible. (We recall attending the wake for a young woman killed in an accident where this idea was also used. Off to the the side of the viewing area a TV screen showed her in the middle of happy activities just weeks earlier.)

We allowed a time during this service when anyone present could pay tribute to Marguerite. The resulting ten or fifteen minutes of outpouring cemented the crowd, many of them strangers to each other, into a body united by once being touched by Marguerite Gibson.

After this we adjourned to the church basement for sandwiches and cookies. This unstructured time allowed many persons to come up to us and say with tears what

Marguerite had meant to them. This time for refreshments put a capstone on the entire event. We all left wanting to live the remaining years of our lives as fully and kindheartedly as had the lovely lady we honored.

Regathering

The family fulfilled Muth's second wish by visiting California when Scott graduated from college in May 1988. There, on the beach in Santa Barbara, Muth's four sons, their wives, and all seven grandchildren formed a circle. We told stories of Muth. We laughed. We cried. *Muth would have loved it.*

Muth had specifically ordained that the highlight of the beach reunion would feature Scott, the graduate and surfer, teaching Bobby, the youngest grandson, to surf. With Scott's help and his proud father videotaping, Bobby got up on a Pacific Ocean wave. We shouted together, "Mission accomplished!" *Muth would have loved it.*

Then we all went down the beach for lunch at the East Beach Grill. We talked and laughed. Later that day we solemnly celebrated Scott's graduation. What a day of memorable tribute! It welded the surviving two generations more solidly to each other than ever before. *Muth would have loved it.*

Grieving and Healing

We, Muth's loved ones, had already grieved for her during her illness, months before her death. Although one is never fully "prepared" for the loss of a family member or close friend, some of the normal stages of mourning may be at least partially resolved before the end comes, if the person is quite elderly and/or terminally ill. We had let go a little bit of Muth at each of a dozen "lasts":

The last time she came to our TV show (late
     September)
The last time she stepped out of the house (October)

The last time she climbed the stairs to her room
(October)

The last time she walked to the bathroom (November)

The last time she got out of bed (November)

The last food she ate—crushed frozen-fruit popsicles
(December)

Looking back at a few of these mileposts, I guess we
sensed at the time she would never do that activity again.
Since we did not know for certain, we always dimly held
the thought that "this is just a temporary setback. She's
healthy. She'll bounce back soon." But we cried many of
our tears at the times when we acknowledged some sad
realities and said such things to each other as, "I have a
feeling that was the last time she will. . . ."

An Afterword

About two weeks before Muth died, Dennis watched a
National Geographic TV special with her. It featured
some beautiful wildlife photography of a family of geese.
They lived in a nest about eight feet above the surface of
a river in Africa. The documentary showed baby goslings
hatching there and followed them as they grew older.
Finally the day came when they left the nest. About a
half-dozen young ones peered out. The mother goose
floated down below, honking, urging them into the big
world.

Dennis and his mother did not merely *watch* this
story, they *lived* it—she the mother goose, he the gosling.
That precious program symbolized much that they had
reminisced about during the preceding weeks. They had
recounted stories of Dennis' first ventures with Mom's
encouragement.

As each little gosling tumbled out of the nest onto the
water, it floated upright and swam over toward its
mother. The last two babies came out together in slow
motion. A half eggshell swept out with them down to the

water. The two goslings swam away, following Mom out of the picture. The inspired photographer zoomed the lens of the camera back to the floating half eggshell, which gradually filled with water and sank below the surface. Dennis told me that this intimate scene said it all for him: "Mom, it's been good. You did your job. That phase of life is done. Thank you and good-bye."

12

Health-Care Management

Dennis and Ruth

Advances in medical science have both lengthened the average life span and made it possible for many in "the senior years" to remain productive, physically active, and mentally alert, well into their eighties and even beyond. Those people so fortunate are often able to be relatively free of the need for direct caregiving by their younger loved ones. Many others—because of general physical decline, mental disorders, or chronic disease—can no longer care for themselves without our help. What then?

The "crisis in health care" we hear so much about today is far broader than the need for funding, although few families can afford the escalating costs of long-term medical or custodial care for their elder members, at least not without outside help. The term *health care* also includes providing appropriate living arrangements for the elderly, whether they live alone, with family, or in a retirement community or nursing home. Therefore, being "parents to our parents" must include helping them plan for the time when they can no longer be completely independent. That means considering the various options available and choosing one *before* an unexpected crisis forces hasty and unwise decisions.

The Crisis

A woman with two kids in high school receives a call from the retirement center in faraway Minnesota where her widowed mother has been living for the past four years. The administrator says, "I'm sorry, Mrs. Jones, but your mother's condition has deteriorated in recent weeks to the point where she cannot take care of herself adequately. She has fallen twice in the past three days and could not get herself off the floor without help. We are not in a position to provide her the surveillance and extra care she needs. You will have to arrange for her to move to a nursing home."

Mrs. Jones takes a crowded few days away from her family to fly up north and look for nursing homes for her elderly mother. She wonders how she will convince Mom, who made her promise four years ago, "You'll never put me in a nursing home." To Mom it meant the same as being condemned to prison.

The daughter discovers that nursing homes cost on the average about $27,000 per year. She wonders how long Mom's meager remaining funds will last. Then what will happen? The Joneses' own finances are already strained. Can this loving daughter consign her proud mother to live off public aid? Mrs. Jones remembers hearing Mom denounce people who lived on public welfare provided by taxpayers' money.

Can she in any way consider taking Mom into her own crowded house? Can she burden her teenagers and busy husband with perhaps years of care for a failing old woman? She feels guilty for hoping that Mom will not live long enough to decline into lower and lower circumstances. She resents her brothers and sisters for not coming forth to offer their help, though they all have ready excuses about busy schedules, limited means, and family obligations.

What Could Have Been the Options?

Life-Care Communities

Mrs. Jones would not be facing the above ordeal if, when Mom picked a retirement center years earlier, she had chosen a life-care community with its own skilled nursing facilities. The administrators would decide when Mom could no longer live in her own apartment. Then they would arrange her transfer to the nursing portion of the community in which she already felt secure. Mom would not in her mind be "shipped off to a nursing home." Instead, she would just live in the more "assisted" living section. In time she might get her bearings again and be able to return to her own apartment. Most likely, prior to needing it permanently, she would have spent several enjoyable intervals in the nursing section. She would not be leaving her friends. They could just walk down the hall or across the grounds to visit with her.

Retirement communities with skilled nursing facilities usually provide continuity of care. They spare the sandwich-years adults from having to transfer into a nursing home a parent who can no longer be independent.

A typical life-care facility provides residents with an apartment, often with a small kitchen and many safety features, such as emergency call buttons. These communities may require a sizable initial investment of capital for use of the apartment, as well as a monthly "maintenance fee" for operating expenses. (The initial sum *may* be refundable if the resident dies or leaves for any reason.) Generally, at least one meal a day is taken in a communal dining room. As mentioned, the best life-care communities have nursing/hospital care on the premises.

Many also have recreational facilities and may provide help with transportation for shopping and other outings.

Nursing Homes

A nursing home operates as a scaled-down hospital. Residents have medical personnel available at all times. Care may be provided on one or more of the following levels:

1. Shelter care. Basically healthy residents receive assistance with only a few things they cannot do for themselves, such as bathing, dressing, or walking.
2. Intermediate care. Residents who have stabilized in a long-term illness or disability receive basic nursing care and restorative services.
3. Skilled nursing care. Residents who can do little or nothing for their own care receive twenty-four-hour surveillance and care by registered nurses, licensed practical nurses, and nurses' aides, as prescribed by a physician. This level of care most nearly represents hospital care. Some residents may temporarily use this level of care to convalesce from surgery, accident, or secondary illness.

Since the premiums for health insurance policies that will cover nursing-home care are very costly, payment for this type of arrangement must usually come from personal and family finances or Medicare and other public funding (there are many restrictions). Geriatric specialists can help with decisions about financing, location, and timing of placement. The local or county health department may have a senior-citizens counselor. Or a particular facility may have a health-care manager available for consultation.

Home Health Care and Support Groups

We in the sandwich years may elect to care for our aging parents in our homes or theirs. In either case, dozens of resources exist to ease our mutual burdens. Some provide practical assistance: transportation, meals brought to the home, housework, "baby-sitting," companionship, and personal care such as bed baths.

Remember, too, the importance of seemingly "minor" services. For example, a beautician's house call can greatly lift the spirits of a housebound elderly woman. And, having someone else take care of the elderly person for a four-hour block of time once a week can bring great relief to the regular caregivers.

Listed below are organizations that may have local chapters to provide services for the aging and their caregivers. The compassionate people in any one of them can usually provide information about other supportive services and personal assistance.

Alzheimer's Disease and Related Disorders Association
American Cancer Society
American Diabetes Association
American Lung Association
American Red Cross
Area Agency on Aging
Arthritis Foundation
Community Nursing Service
Easter Seal Center
Family Service Association
FISH
National Kidney Foundation
Salvation Army
United Parkinson's Foundation

You might find the greatest help from a home-health-care coordinator recommended by your parent's or your own local physician. We patronize a large medical clinic that has its own home-health-care coordinator, a gold mine of information, and caring energy. Many churches have a Stephen Ministry or a Caring Community or a parish nurse. If your church does not, consider starting such a program.

Hospice programs often tie in with a whole network of caring agencies and persons. Another resource is your county health department, which probably has at least one person who knows where to find help for senior citizens in the community. Finally, if your parent is hospitalized, be aware that most hospitals have a social-service department or discharge planner. These assistants can put patients and their families in touch with support groups for everything from colostomies to Alzheimer's to depression.

Suppose that your parent lives far away or that you plan to go out of town for many days. You would want someone to call your parent once or more each day just for reassurance. The Red Cross offers Telecare, a program that does just that.

Another type of telephone service is called Lifeline (in our area). Variations exist under other names in other parts of the country. Elderly persons who subscribe to this service receive a small wireless push-button signaling device to wear as a necklace or bracelet. In an emergency, the wearer pushes the button to activate a communication unit connected to the nearest telephone. (Hospital volunteers install these units for a subscriber.) The unit automatically dials a twenty-four-hour response center at the hospital, where specially trained operators immediately retrieve information about the subscriber and send an emergency responder to the home.

Your local library may have a list of services for seniors or at least may offer, "I know just the person you should talk to." This informal kind of connection will probably meet your needs most satisfactorily. As another resource, don't overlook the American Association for Retired Persons (AARP). They offer abundant valuable information in their magazine, *Modern Maturity*. Members can also get prescription medications by mail, usually at a discount. (Sandwich-years people notice: you can join when you're only fifty!)

All of the above organizations offer helpful printed information. They also sponsor (or can recommend) support groups where the aging and their caregivers can socialize and encourage each other. There are other groups for family members of disabled or terminally ill individuals.

Legal Arrangements

You can save yourself later complications if you convince your parents of the need to execute two documents *before* they become incapacitated.

First, *each* of them should draw up a will that specifies their wishes for distribution of financial assets/material possessions and names an executor. A "last will and testament" may also contain instructions as to funeral and burial arrangements. However, since reading of the will is sometimes delayed until *after* the funeral, some prefer to specify these wishes in a separate, less formal "letter." Even for a "simple" will, it is a good idea to consult a lawyer regarding its terms, since state laws vary as to inheritance rights and just what is (and is not) legal. (See also chapter 15.)

Second, each of your parents should have an attorney's assistance in drawing up a Durable Power of Attorney.

This document authorizes someone else to implement the individual's wishes if he or she becomes incompetent, including empowering an agent to manage one's financial affairs. Depending on the state of residency, it also may work better than a living will to specify who shall decide (and on what basis) when to terminate "extraordinary" life-support measures.

Permanent Disabilities

Long-term care becomes a major consideration with such chronic, degenerative conditions as Alzheimer's,

Parkinson's, multiple sclerosis, diabetes, stroke, and respiratory disabilities. For example . . .

Stroke. The Anderson kids had always known their father as a strong man who made all the decisions in the family and brought home the paycheck. After his stroke they could hardly bear to see him stumbling around, drooling from his mask-like face, spilling his food so that someone else had to feed him. They felt a mixture of pity and disgust toward Dad, anger toward God, and guilt about these negative feelings.

Dad's stroke cost a lot of money. He went into a hospital for about a week, but Medicare regulations would not let him stay any longer. He was not in that small percentage of elderly persons who have full insurance coverage. What Medicare did *not* cover—but which seemed essential for proper diagnosis and treatment planning—ended up costing the Anderson family $10,000. Most of that paid for several intricate test procedures and consultations from medical specialists.

Then a consultant from a rehabilitation center said their program could help this stroke victim. They took Dad as an inpatient for an intensive six-week program to restore as much physical functioning as possible. That cost the family another $30,000. Then Dad came home— still far from his old self.

Some of the Anderson children lived far enough away to incur substantial costs traveling to see their disabled dad. They felt guilty for not coming more often, and not doing more. Ones who lived closer spent time away from their own families and responsibilities. For the first month, they did it joyfully (or at least out of pity). After that it started to wear thin, and they found themselves continuing the actions but with corrosive inner feelings of obligation and resentment.

Parkinson's Disease. This affliction involves a degeneration of one specific part of the brain. The mental processes usually stay clear, but varying sections of the body become "stiff," as rigidity affects muscles and joints.

Since the person's face may lose its expressiveness, loved ones get the mistaken impression that sufferers are not "with it," though they are. As one of the first signs, penmanship becomes constricted. Next the person's walk is characterized by a stuttering, shuffling gait. A pill-rolling kind of tremor seizes the hands and fingers, especially under tension. Parkinson's patients can carry on intelligible conversations, but their voice tone loses its animation as rigidity spreads to the face and mouth. In later stages, the increasing rigidity and tremors can cause difficulties in locomotion, dressing, and even eating. Treatment varies, but is usually only partly successful in controlling some of the symptoms, and not in all patients.

Alzheimer's Disease. Old psychiatric manuals referred to this condition as "pre-senile dementia." This means that the individuals so afflicted seem "old before their time." Brain tissue ages more rapidly than usual, first affecting memory functions, particularly short-term memory. Patients in the early stages may clearly remember their first day in school, but not what they had for breakfast an hour ago.

(Ruth's cousin, Lois, showed the first signs of forgetfulness at about age fifty. She became disoriented while out driving and pulled off the road. When police came to assist her, they saw the address on her driver's license and escorted her home. Then they called her next of kin. Thus began a long series of such incidents, calling for difficult decisions among the children, with Lois's own role in the decision-making unclear.)

As the disease progresses, mental deterioration becomes more and more apparent. Verbal skills fade and speech becomes labored and confused. The patient is often "hostile" and exhibits antisocial behavior, even toward loved ones who are trying to help. Eventually, most Alzheimer's victims are unable to care for themselves and do not recognize family, friends, and once-familiar surroundings. As they truly become "babies" again, they will require constant supervision as well as utmost patience.

Caring for these patients is a full-time responsibility, a task that exacts a tremendous physical and emotional toll on spouses and other loved ones who try to do so in their own homes. Many caregivers find this impossible without some outside help. For some, placing a loved one in a suitable nursing facility may be the best course, although this is a difficult decision for family members. It may also produce inappropriate guilt feelings about not being able to handle things themselves. However, since present Medicare funding and most health-insurance plans do not cover expenses for "custodial care," the expenses involved may be insurmountable for the average family.

It is very important that a suspected Alzheimer's patient be properly diagnosed and continue under the care of a physician, both to rule out any other possible causes and to have available feedback on how to handle the ramifications of the disease. Although medical personnel continue to search for the causes and effective treatment for Alzheimer's, results to date are inconclusive and, at best, only slightly encouraging. Until more is known about the disease, efforts must be concentrated on helping the victims' families cope with the affliction without exhausting their own financial and emotional resources and physical well-being.

An Afterword

The "case descriptions" above are unpleasant but realistic reminders of the types of disablement that may further complicate the "parenting of parents" responsibilities for people in the sandwich years. There are no easy solutions for those called on to be caregivers in situations that place such a massive strain on a family's financial, mental, and emotional resources.

If you are a member of such a burdened family, it is

vital for your own health that you make every possible use of the community resources outlined previously in this chapter. If, on the other hand, you are not directly involved, but are a friend, fellow parishioner, and/or neighbor of a caregiver for a chronically disabled relative, be cheerfully available to lend your practical and emotional support. This means *not* waiting to be called on, but volunteering your help for such "ordinary" things as grocery shopping or providing some free time for the caregiver by "baby-sitting" the patient for a few hours.

Part Three

Spousal Concerns in the Sandwich Years

13

Shifting Gears

Dennis

We all had a wonderful time the year Ruth and I shared Christmas break in Florida with our college-aged sons. Then we said a heartfelt good-bye to the boys at the Fort Lauderdale airport and had to wait a couple of hours before our plane left for Chicago.

I soon began noticing little mannerisms about Ruth that somehow jarred my preference for neatness and precision. For example, she handed me the envelope containing our airline tickets, and I noticed that she had the ticket inside the envelope upside down. I noticed that she had set our carry-on luggage on the "wrong" side of our seat in the waiting area—the left instead of the right! When I commented on these "infractions," Ruth apologized. Somehow I felt that she did not mean her apology, so I confronted her on what I regarded as still another error. Tension crackled between us.

Suddenly a light flashed in Ruth's eyes and she smiled

as she said, "Dennis, do you know what is happening with us?" I answered that all I could recognize was that *she* was being unreasonable and a bit annoying. Ruth patiently commented, "No, we are simply merging traffic."

Rediscovering Each Other

Cars entering a freeway use a merging lane to blend their speed with the flow of traffic. Merging traffic in this orderly fashion makes for fewer collisions than if vehicles were to enter after making a sharp turn from a dead stop. Over the years, we had used "merging traffic" as a shorthand term to describe the friction we sometimes experienced when getting back together after a time apart. It had become our warning signal, a reminder to take pains to rediscover each other's experiences, feelings, and thoughts.

At first it seemed ridiculous to me to refer to this time in Fort Lauderdale as "merging traffic." If anything, I thought, Ruth and I had been *too much* together for the past intense week.

But Ruth explained her insight: "We have been together a lot recently. However, we have been focusing our energy and attention on the boys. We have immersed ourselves in the joys of being Mom and Dad. Now we must merge traffic again, but as husband and wife." I thought a moment and then said, "I think you're right."

Ruth got to the heart of the matter when she sensitively asked, "How are you feeling about saying good-bye to the boys?" Tears filled my eyes when I said, "I will really miss them." My irritability had been an indirect expression of my sadness about saying good-bye to our sons. Like most people, I find it difficult to shift gears back into the routine of life. In my mind, Ruth represented something of an intruder just then, as if *she* had driven the boys away from me.

The opportunity to express my sadness freed me to appreciate my life partner once again. We had emptied our nest six months earlier, when our youngest son left for college. We had adjusted fairly well to that, but now we had to adjust *again*. Our joyful family visit had temporarily filled the nest, which meant that we had to handle our conflicted feelings once more.

A Collision of Expectations

It helped us both to resolve this tension at the airport when we recalled the earlier clash in which we first recognized the concept of merging traffic.

The Setting

One summer we spent a delightful family vacation with friends at a camp in the north woods. Ruth had gone north first with our youngest son, and I came up a few days later with the two older boys, after they finished another activity. During those days that I sat in my office, I dreamed of the peace and quiet and solitude of the woods. I could hardly wait to get to the outdoors and commune with a birch tree.

Meanwhile, Ruth, already at the camp, could hardly wait for me to arrive so she could introduce me to all the interesting people she was meeting. Ruth was enjoying her flitting from table to table during mealtimes and coffee breaks. She poured herself into making new friends and telling them how much they would "enjoy her fine husband."

The long-awaited day arrived. When the older boys and I pulled into the camp, Ruth immediately whisked me off to a coffee time and began introducing me to one person after another. "This is my husband I was telling you about," she would excitedly burst out to people. No doubt she sensed an unspoken reluctance from me. In fact, if you take a trip up to this camp, you will probably notice my heel marks gouged permanently into the trails. I certainly dragged my feet!

In Ruth's eyes, I was raining on her parade, spoiling her

fun, acting like a stick-in-the-mud. To my point of view, Ruth was bombarding me with social obligations I had not invited. I saw her as wrenching me away from my beloved woods, forcing me to do more of what I did when *not* on vacation. I did not want to make small talk with people, smiling at them, inquiring about their backgrounds and lives. I wanted time *alone.*

The Problem

We had two perfectly justifiable agendas. For Ruth, a vacation meant a wonderful opportunity to meet and enjoy people. For me, it meant I would have time alone to enjoy the outdoors and God's refreshing creation. And this particular location held great symbolic meaning for me.

At this place as a camper, two days before my thirteenth birthday, I first clearly heard and understood the simple Bible message that the God who created me loved me and provided a way through Christ that I could become personally connected to him. By opening my heart to receive Jesus Christ as my Savior, Lord, and Friend, I said yes to God's offer of eternal life and became a new person. For me, to visit this camp meant to recapture that experience, and I wanted time in which nothing else distracted me.

We often see in the couples we counsel that what originally drew them to each other later becomes the source of greatest friction. The very qualities that attracted Ruth and myself to each other collided at that camp. I loved Ruth's outgoing effervescence and social competence. Ruth had many times told me that she admired my "depth," my meditative earnestness about things of God. Each of us expected the other to support those qualities, not oppose them, so now we had to take time to iron out this collision of expectations.

We took a couple of hours apart from other people and went off to a secluded cabin to discuss our differences one at a time. But we did not really *feel* like doing it. Although we knew the skills to use because we taught them to other people, skill is no use without the will. We *chose* to communicate with each other because we considered it a part of our wedding vows. Our hearts were not in it!

When we began talking about our collision, each of us wanted to talk first. We quickly realized that there would be no communication as long as we had two talkers and no listener, so one of us would have to volunteer to listen first. That often presents a pride-based stalemate between spouses who are angry at each other. Each wants to force the other to "see reason" by being the first to tell his or her version of the situation.

Two people stuck in this kind of deadlock resemble trailer trucks approaching each other on a one-lane mountain road. Neither can continue its journey until one of them backs up to a wide spot in the road. Each driver initially leans out the window and shakes his fist at the other or blows his horn as a useless threat to make the other give way. When both drivers think that backing up would represent an act of weakness, they lose sight of their journey in a power struggle to conquer the opponent.

The Solution

The Bible offers good news with practical implications for precisely the type of stand-off these mythical truck drivers face. Near the end of his brilliant reasoning in Romans 8, the apostle Paul offers the concept "more than conquerors." Think about it. The truck driver who first backs up to a wide spot in the road makes movement possible. Instead of conquering an enemy, he defeats the sticky situation that has paralyzed them both. Similarly, the marital partner who rushes to do the first listening makes possible the two-way communication that can resolve most conflict.

Who should listen first? Should the wife humble herself in this way because Scripture urges her to submit to her husband? Or should the husband take this initiative because Scripture urges him to live with his wife in an understanding way and to love her as Christ loved the church? Christ's love for the church, his bride, moved him to sacrifice his very *life* for her.

I believe it's the man's move first. To be "manly" means to shoulder the more difficult burdens, and we all find it hard to delay speaking our minds. That's tough enough to qualify as "man's work." Let Christian husbands readily accept the miniature death of pride that comes in humbling themselves and drawing out their wives' thoughts, feelings, and opinions in a disagreement.

Ruth agrees that husbands ought to take that initiative, but she adds that if the man does not think of it, the woman should rush to be the first listener. Someone needs to do it. In the Christian view of things it is not a defeat but an honor to be the first listener and thus make communication possible.

The Application

I began that long-ago conversation in the remote cabin as follows:

> Ruth, before I tell you my thoughts and my feelings in this difficulty between us, I want to be sure that I understand how you're seeing things. I think that you feel deeply disappointed at my lack of interest in the social agenda that you had in mind. You may feel frustrated by my pulling away from these situations in which you are trying to introduce me to other people. Maybe you even feel kind of betrayed. Am I reading you right?

To help me take this godly position that I did not *feel* like taking, I visualized myself as a physician assisting Ruth to give birth to a baby: her thoughts and feelings in this situation. I saw her viewpoint as a fragile, precious, living thing, so I took pains to help her express it in words. Textbooks refer to this procedure as "active listening." It required my full involvement, including eye contact with Ruth and an earnest desire to see through her eyes, whether or not I agreed with her perception of the situation. I did not just "endure" her presentation of her thoughts, resentfully waiting for her to finish so that I could get in a rebuttal. Rather, I sought to lay the first plank in a bridge of understanding.

Ruth played her part by saying, "Yes, that's exactly how I feel. Furthermore. . . . " She welcomed this opportunity to unburden herself of the painful emotions that she had been feeling but had not quite verbalized until now. In doing so, she was expressing trust in her husband, which an alienated wife would not do. Too often, spouses in this situation bitterly clam up with such comments as these:

"If you really cared about me, you would know what I'm thinking without my having to tell you."
"I can't talk with someone who's been as rude to me as you've been."
"Don't try to kid me. You're not really interested."
"Don't you think it's a little late? Let's just forget it."

Ruth unburdened herself of her thoughts and feelings about what happened between us. She took pains not to belittle me or make any condemning remarks about me as a person. She clearly and emphatically told of her own frustration, hurt, loneliness, and disappointment. I *listened* to her, which was the first step in showing that I wanted to understand.

Then Ruth gave me an opportunity to unburden myself about how I viewed what was happening. She maintained eye contact with me and did not interrupt until I had finished expressing myself clearly but cordially. Then she restated in her words her understanding of what I was trying to get across. Going back and forth in this way, we soon came to see how each of us had worthy expectations that were simply different.

The Results

It did not take long for us to devise a compromise that worked well for the rest of the week. I would come to each coffee hour and meal and let Ruth introduce me to anyone she wanted to. I agreed to be sociable and not sulk during this process. In turn, Ruth gave her blessing to my choice to spend the other times doing whatever I wanted to do. She recognized that I would come back a better man from having spent time alone in the woods.

We learned from this collision of wills the valuable lesson about merging traffic. We now realize that when we come together after having been apart for even a short time, we often have a new perspective, including different expectations for our relationship. It is then that we need to merge traffic like cars entering a freeway. We do that by taking turns asking, "What's been going on with you? Do you want to unload? How are you feeling?" By updating each other on significant experiences and what they mean to us, we make plain in words what we would each like from the other. And the traffic keeps moving in the direction of marital harmony!

Reducing Friction

Two Strategies

Having kids around usually provides enough distraction that spouses do not notice all the flaws in each other. When the kids leave home, the spouses begin noticing previously invisible shortcomings. There are two strategies people use to reduce friction over another's imperfections. We can (1) try to change the other person (by making requests or persuading—and increasing the pressure as necessary); or (2) change ourselves (by reviewing our attitudes to see if we can scale down from "demands" to "preferences").

The Serenity Prayer used by Alcoholics Anonymous and other self-help groups summarizes these two strategies as follows: "God, grant me the serenity to accept the things I cannot change, courage to change the things I can, and wisdom to know the difference."

Application

For years there was friction in our household over how Ruth started the car. I had given precise instructions for the process. I wanted her to pump the gas before turning the key in the ignition and then to stop turning the key the instant the engine had begun running. Repeatedly, I implored Ruth to follow my procedure. I demonstrated it to her as I sat her in the driver's seat and supervised her going through the steps precisely. I even wrote the instructions on a note and taped it to the dashboard. Nothing worked. Ruth continued to start the car in ways that grated on my nerves like fingernails screeching on a chalkboard.

Did I decide to handle this problem by hiding the car keys? Of course not! I applied the Serenity Prayer. I had tried "courage" (even belligerence) to change Ruth. "Wisdom" now said that the time had come to "accept" Ruth's way of starting the car. But I wondered how I could possibly do this without denying my feelings, trying to suppress them, only to have them bubble up from deep pools of resentment.

I finally decided to do some visualization therapy on myself. I imagined that Ruth had suddenly died in a tragic accident. I next pictured myself sitting alone in the house, aching over my loss of Ruth and yearning for just one more chance to tell her how much I loved her. Finally I imagined an angel appearing before me and saying, "Your wish has been granted. You will be allowed two minutes with Ruth—on one condition: you must permit her to spend the first minute starting your car in the driveway. Do you accept?"

I imagined myself enthusiastically answering, "Oh, yes, by all means!" Then, as I heard Ruth starting the car in the driveway, it was music to my ears. It meant that my darling was back in my life, and in a matter of seconds would be in my arms.

Results

Having used this way of thinking, I asked myself, "Does she have to die and return from the dead before you regard her way of starting the car as a welcome sound?" In that moment I was transformed by the renewing of my mind, as the Scripture teaches in Romans 12:2. I took a new view of her habit—as a *mannerism*, not an annoyance. I saw it as part of her signature, a mark of her individuality. Most of all, I saw it as proof positive that she was alive and well and part of my life. Now I wholeheartedly tell Ruth, "Honey, you can start the car any way you want to!"

We can reduce the friction over what we perceive as faults of our loved ones by attaching new meaning to old annoyances. If we can view a minor imperfection as simply that person's identifying mark, we can think how much we would miss even that hallmark if the person were no longer around. Here we have an alternative to denial and repression of our negative feelings.

An Afterword

An "empty nest" presents new challenges in any marriage. But it need not mean "mid-life crisis." In a relationship built on love, respect, and commitment, there are mutual goals, though each partner may prefer a different route or speed level. If you remember that you are both heading in the same general direction, it will be easier to merge traffic, even if one or the other needs to yield the right-of-way temporarily.

Open communication—correctly interpreting the words and actions of a loved one—eases the traffic flow and forestalls dangerous collisions. By keeping open the lines of verbal give-and-take, we can reach new understanding and a satisfactory resolution of conflict, which leads us into the next chapter. . . .

14

Marital Communication

Ruth

Some years ago we heard Dr. David Augsburger speak about techniques for achieving good human relations. He explained that the labels we apply to the words and actions of other people represent a choice that we make. The labels then determine how we feel and act toward these persons.

"Labeling"—we do it all the time. For example, think of all the labels you can apply to this page. You can call it information, a black-and-white design, the written word, a commercial product, a publication, communication, English language, literature. But how would you answer a person who asks you which of those is the one and only correct label for what you are seeing? You would probably groan and answer, "All of the above!" Of course! What you see in front of you, not just now but *all* the time, could be called by many different names. The name you choose depends on the purpose you have in mind. In turn, this label determines how you relate to what you see.

Relabeling

Application

Dennis and I had occasion to put the labeling idea to use within thirty minutes of leaving Dr. Augsburger's lecture. We left with Dennis driving the car and me riding beside him. It was a snowy night. When Dennis got a little closer behind the car ahead of us than I felt comfortable with, I grimaced. Then I gasped and braced my arms against the dashboard and my feet against the floorboards. I periodically made comments like, "Aren't you a little too close? You're going too fast! Didn't you take that last corner a little too abruptly?" Dennis's sighs and body language signaled his anger at my remarks and gestures. He could not see these as anything other than "criticism," a label that made him feel defensive and resentful—though I didn't understand that *yet*.

Finally Dennis said to me, "I wonder if you can help me apply what Dr. Augsburger was talking about. Here we are having a terribly tense time with each other. I feel like I am driving safely, but you continue to squirm and comment and bombard me with disapproval. Since I am having a hard time seeing what you're doing as anything but criticism, I feel very distant and alienated from you. Can you help me to see this in any different way?"

I paused a moment and then said softly, "Well, maybe it will help if I give you an I-message." (This is a standard technique from communications training. When you confront people about behavior on their part that you do not like, begin your statement with the pronoun "I" instead of "you." Starting with "you" tends to create a statement that sounds like blaming, such as, "You are driving like a maniac.") Now *I* could explain: "I am feeling scared when it is snowing outside and our car starts to tailgate the car ahead of us. I fear that we might get into an accident. I would like it if you would slow down and keep a little more distance between our car and the next one."

As Dennis listened intently for a different way to label my words and actions, a particular phrase stood out. My words, "I would like," triggered a flash of insight in Dennis's mind: *"Request*—she is making a request." The instant that he could use the label "request" as an alternative for "criticism," he visibly relaxed and his jaw muscles unclenched. He told me later that he felt a surge of affection for me and immediately *wanted* to slow down.

In a matter of seconds, Dennis slowed down. He said to me, "How does this seem, honey? Does this feel more comfortable to you?" This gracious action on his part so moved me that I burst into tears of relief saying, "Thank you, Denny, thank you so much."

What We Learned

When we discussed this incident, I realized that as long as Dennis viewed my words and actions simply as "criticism," he could think of only two responses. He could either give in like an unmanly wimp (and harbor a grudge) or get aggressive and intimidate me into docility. When he recognized that I was making "a request," it freed him to act like a gentleman. (Wimps give in to a tyrant's criticism; gentlemen grant the requests of others.)

Dennis prides himself on being a caring individual, which includes wanting any passengers in his car to feel comfortable. He explained that with the label "request," it dawned on him that he could bring peace of mind to the person dearest to him. He could make me feel safe simply by lifting the ball of his foot a quarter-inch! And *I* learned something, too—I should have made clear my "request" in the first place!

In this example, Dennis was transformed by "the renewing of his mind." By finding an alternative, valid label for the behavior of our loved ones, we redirect our thoughts and reactions. This instance had a permanent effect on both of us. We have never again had a conflict over my feelings about Dennis's driving.

Now, when I object to some aspect of Dennis's driving, I try to be more diplomatic. And Dennis, instead of taking it as "criticism" and hardening himself against it, receives it as a "request." He willingly adjusts his driving so that I feel comfortable. (Dennis says that when he drives alone he follows his own preferences, always staying within the law, of course.)

Marital Metaphors

Rubber Marriages

All marriages need to have the qualities of rubber. First of all, rubber is *resilient* and *elastic.* It bounces back when stress bends it out of shape, and it expands to fit irregular surfaces. Spouses need to do that with each other. Sometimes our partner seems to be strangely inconsiderate and irrational. We need to bounce back from the hurts and disappointments inevitable in any close relationship, realizing that neither of us is perfect. The love that underlies a marital commitment can stretch around bumps in the road.

Rubber also *erases* mistakes. In rubber marriages, the partners stand ready to forgive the mistakes and hurts inflicted by their mates. (In this process, the flexible quality of rubber also comes into play.) But forgiveness must not be a mere whitewash based on the pretense that either the wrong did not happen or that it did not matter to the injured one. Here we draw a distinction between "forgiveness" and "reconciliation." We can *forgive* someone without that person's participation if we conduct a transaction between ourselves and God, letting go of our bitterness or hurt toward the person who wronged us. *Reconciliation* requires the participation of both parties. You resume normal relations only after the one who has inflicted the hurt acknowledges his or her wrong and repents of it. That means saying, "I was wrong," in one way or another and implying that the offense will not be repeated.

For reconciliation to occur, the offenders must indicate what they would do differently if they had the situation to live over again. (The injured party must also be willing to acknowledge that he or she is not entirely blameless.) Without this kind of rethinking, a couple leaves open the likelihood of a repetition. Sometimes people give an empty apology after hurting a loved one. They merely say quickly, "I'm sorry," in a hurry to have the issue dropped and to move on as if nothing unusual happened. If we put this irresponsible attitude into words, it translates into the following sentence: "I want you to be friendly with me again even though I reserve the right to abuse you in the future as I have in the past."

Broken Bones Get Stronger

During the years of high school sports, one of our sons broke a leg. The physician showed us an Xray at the time of the break. Eight weeks later he let us compare a new Xray with the old one. We saw from the Xrays that the healed bone actually had a greater thickness at the point where it broke than did the neighboring bone tissue. We were told that if the leg ever broke again, it would break anywhere but the place where it had previously broken.

When spouses in a rubber marriage hurt each other and then thoroughly talk through the hurt and reconcile over it, they create a learning experience by erasing the *negative* effects of the hurt. It makes them less likely to repeat that hurt than before. In the written Chinese language, the picture word for "crisis" consists of two other words combined: "danger" and "opportunity." To keep marriages healthy, couples can turn every crisis of hurt and disappointment into an opportunity to learn, grow, improve, and draw still closer to each other.

Poking Some Air Holes

In the Arctic Ocean, seals can swim under water for many minutes. However, since they do not have gills, they must come up periodically for air. Living under thick ice, they need to have air holes through the ice in several places. To keep these vital holes from freezing over, a seal visits each one frequently enough to poke its nose through the thin crust of ice that has begun to form.

Couples need to keep open their lines of communication by frequent attention to any icy barriers that begin to develop between them. If either one feels any kind of wall developing, it is time to comment on the fact. Simple comments do the job: "Martha, I'm not sure why, but I'm feeling some kind of tension going on between us. Let's talk about it." Or: "Fred, I'm starting to feel myself pulling away from you emotionally. I don't want to do that. So I would like you to help me with this. What do you think is going on?"

The survival techniques used by seals illustrate the powerful scriptural principle in Ephesians 4:26: "Do not let the sun go down while you are still angry." To say that another way, keep your irritations no bigger than twenty-four-hour-sized. Deal with them before they freeze so thick and hard that you can't bump your nose through them.

The Sorry Chair

In the cheese country of southern Wisconsin lies a tourist attraction known as "Little Norway." It is not a town, but a farm settled by Norwegian immigrants over one hundred years ago. A tour guide once took us around the interesting buildings on this lovely spot of land.

She walked us up one flight to the master bedroom of the main log farmhouse. Near the marriage bed stood an unusual piece of furniture, which our guide referred to as "the sorry chair." It was a small, low seat of hardwood set in the corner of the bedroom. We noticed that it was just barely big enough for two people to squeeze a portion of their posteriors onto.

Our guide explained the custom. If the husband and wife ever went to their bedroom angry at each other, they had to sit together on that uncomfortable chair until they both said, "I'm sorry." Until that healing gesture, they could not go to bed. These Norwegians took seriously that biblical principle of not letting the sun go down on their "wrath" (to put it in King James English). They literally built into the furniture of their home a principle that would keep them communicating with each other. It would be physically uncomfortable to stay emotionally alienated for long.

About Finances

Couples often come for counseling because of serious problems about spending. Typically, one feels that the other spends too much without consulting him or her. In that case we ask partners to think silently of a dollar figure above which they would like the spouse to consult them *before* spending. A husband might say he wants his wife to check with him before buying anything over twenty dollars. His wife might fix on thirty dollars as the limit he can spend without her consent. They might compromise on twenty-five as the ceiling they will both observe.

This agreement does not apply to routine purchases like groceries, but it serves to curb impulsive spending for items that the family might better do without. To motivate this kind of thrift in our own household, we make a game of seeing how often we can turn down things we would like to buy. Sometimes we add the extra incentive of putting that amount instead toward some larger project that strongly matters to us.

We find that many couples we counsel do not understand what the word *budget* means. They usually define it according to some vague but negative concept of "tightening our belts." However, as a verb, "budget" is *positive* and refers to allocating resources according to certain priorities. As a noun, "a budget" refers to a written plan by which the couple decides how much of their dependable income will go into each of several expense areas. On seeing how much *must* go toward such fixed expenses as mortgage, transportation, and groceries, the couple can decide how much they have left over for "extras."

Some couples confuse "extras" with "necessities." A few think they *must* move to a larger house. Others would consider periodic vacationing in a tropical paradise as vital to their well-being. We find a scriptural guideline that helps us decide where to spend money. Since Romans 13:8 teaches us to keep out of debt, we pass up anything we would have to buy on credit.

An Afterword

Current divorce statistics confirm our observation that couples today—especially in the sandwich years, when the children are grown—increasingly regard a legal end to their marriage as the way out of a painful relationship. In certain circumstances, especially where long-term and fla-grant adultery or abuse is involved, separation may be the best course, at least temporarily. However, no breakup should be finalized unless the couple has made a sincere attempt to resolve their differences less drastically.

As we counsel couples in fragmented marriages, we urge them to salvage the love on which they first made their commitment to remain together "for better or for worse." Often they find new ways to weather the "worse." With that approach, if a couple still opts for divorce, it is sometimes possible for them to reconcile later and build a new marriage with each other that is better and stronger than the first one. For this important new beginning, we rec-ommend reviewing the distinction between "forgiveness" and "reconciliation." Dennis spells this out more fully in two chapters of his book *The Strong-Willed Adult* (Baker Book House, 1987).

For further background on divorce and remarriage, we recommend two particularly well-done books:

Jay E. Adams, *Marriage, Divorce and Remarriage* (Grand Rapids: Baker Book House, 1980). This provides many practical applica-tions of soundly reasoned biblical arguments.

William Luck, *Divorce and Remarriage* (San Francisco: Harper and Row, 1987). Subtitled "Recovering the biblical view," this book is a thorough, scholarly approach to the subject.

15

Retirement Planning

Ruth

Dennis once commented to me that many airline pilots love their work so much that they can hardly imagine life without flying. They let the years creep up on them and catch them off guard. One day they are flying a 747 to London. A few days later they have landed *as a passenger* in St. Petersburg and are playing shuffleboard with other retirees.

Except when unexpected illness cuts short one's normal working years, retirement should come as no surprise. Any landing can be bumpy if not anticipated, and we have heard some alarming statistics about career-happy people who have not readied themselves for the later years. Many die in something like a year and a half or endure a living death of bored unhappiness. By contrast, others see retirement coming and start practicing little pieces of it a few years ahead. They live many productive and enjoyable years after retiring because they have planned for them.

Mental preparation plays a large role in adjusting to our final years. We also face some practical considerations: the financial, legal, and logistical aspects of retirement. Checking our instruments and planning our descent will ease the landing process.

Financial Planning

The Social Security Administration gives the following approximate figures concerning sources of financial support for Americans on reaching age sixty-five:

45% depend (at least in part) on relatives
30% live on charity
23% continue working
2% live independently, off savings and pensions

Those who make up the 2 percent have done so by advanced planning and by carefully protecting their assets. Most find that their best investment was a home that they bought and watched appreciate in value over the years. They face one problem with assets tied up in real estate, however. It may be hard to sell profitably if the market is temporarily down when they need to convert to assets that pay regular dividends for daily living expenses.

Space limitations prevent a complete discussion here of the many factors involved in planning for one's future financial security. Matters to be considered include employment-related pension plans, tax-deferred investments such as IRA's and Keogh plans, long-term investment in securities, and health-insurance protection that will supplement Medicare benefits. It is never too early to begin this planning, and there are many self-help books on the subject. If you want professional advice, ask your attorney, a business associate, and/or trusted family friend to recommend an accredited financial counselor.

Self-employed as we are, we have our own professional

corporation pay for insurance on Dennis's life. In the event of his death, the insurance proceeds will adequately support me. If we both live well into retirement, the cash value of that life insurance will form a major portion of our assets. Also, in these ten to fifteen years preceding our retirement, we are concentrating on saving the major portion of the money we will need to live on after retiring.

Living Arrangements

In chapter 12 we described "retirement communities." From what we know so far, we favor a life-care option for most retirees. Eligibility usually starts at age sixty, but some persons in their early sixties feel stifled by the preponderance of inactive, much older neighbors. (On the other hand, these centers will accept only persons who can transport themselves under their own power.) The important thing is to plan ahead so that you are not forced into a hasty relocation by a sudden change in circumstances.

We often hear older persons debating about whether to relocate to a sunny climate or stay among known places and people. We presently look forward to living in a pleasant facility in our already-familiar area. We can have "Florida" indoors, all through a northern winter.

Legal Matters

Leaving a Will

If you do not specify ahead of time how you wish your assets distributed upon your death, your loved ones may experience delays and other difficulties when your estate is probated. Spare them that added pain by indicating in writing how your estate will pass on and who you wish to serve as executor. See an attorney *now* to draw up a will that clearly states your intentions (some of which may not be feasible under the laws of your state). Generally, each spouse should have a separate will. If your assets are substantial, you may want advice on how certain trust arrangements can facilitate their transfer and minimize the tax bite. (For more on this subject, see chapter 12.)

Durable Power of Attorney

A will specifies what happens to your belongings when you die. A Durable Power of Attorney spells out who should do what with your affairs in the event you become incapacitated. With it you can specify a person to act as your agent and make decisions for you when you cannot. Once you have signed this document, make sure you have plenty of conversations with that person so that he or she clearly understands your wishes. This includes making decisions about life-support measures if medical experts declare you terminally ill and you become unconscious. This matter is sometimes covered in a "living will," but state laws differ on what this may legally cover.

Tell Where to Find What

As executor for the estates of his mother and father, Dennis had to sort through scattered records to find the documents he needed. These experiences taught him the value of preparing clear instructions and a "location list" for loved ones, especially the estate's executor. Accordingly he wrote out a list of "Items My Wife or Other Executor Should Know at My Death." The following shows some of the items Dennis mentioned:

1. Copies of my will, marriage license, home mortgage, birth certificate, and other documents are in safe deposit box #____ at ____ Bank's main office. My key for this box is in my top dresser drawer under my jewelry box.
2. Insurance policies and other important papers are kept in the black zippered leather pouch in the upper-left-hand corner of my closet at home.

3. Tax records can be found in two files: (a) second drawer of the far-left filing cabinet in Room #4 at the office; (b) older ones in the second drawer of the filing cabinet in our upstairs office at home.

4. Vehicle titles are in the file folder marked "CAR" in the top file drawer at home.

5. First mortgage on our home is #_____ , held by _____ Savings and Loan.

6. If I die while on commercial transportation that I purchased with my First National VISA card, they will pay $100,000 to my estate.

Dennis gave a copy of this list to me, put another into our safe deposit box, and sent a copy to each of our children. That increases the chances that someone will find a copy in the event that we lose our own copies or that we die at the same time.

De-cluttering Our Lives

When our children finally do have to sort through our things after our death, we want them to encounter as little inconvenience and embarrassment as possible. That means we must rid ourselves of clutter, starting now.

Clutter's Last Stand—what a great book title! Don Aslett wrote it, and it was published by Writer's Digest Books (Cincinnati, 1984). This book entertained us while revolutionizing our lives. We show below a sample from "Some Junk-Sorting Guidelines."

It Is Junk If:

It's broken or obsolete (and fixing it is unrealistic)
You've outgrown it, physically or emotionally
You've always hated it
It's the wrong size, wrong color, or wrong style
Using it is more bother than it's worth
It generates bad feelings

You have to clean it, store it, and insure it (but you
   don't get much use or enjoyment out of it)
It will shock, bore, or burden the coming generation

It's Not Junk If It:
Generates love and good feelings
Helps you make a living
Will do something you need done
Has significant cash value
Gives you more than it takes
Will enrich or delight the coming generation

Dennis considers *The Celebration of Discipline* by
Richard J. Foster (New York: Harper and Row, 1978) one
of the most valuable books he has ever read. Foster enti-
tles one chapter "The Discipline of Simplicity." Yes, it
takes self-discipline for us to say "No" to many good
things, so we can say "Yes" to a few *excellent* things.
This applies to material objects and to how we use our
time. We do better to travel light!

Dennis learned the freedom of simplicity when he
underwent a seventeen-day wilderness course similar to
Outward Bound. The program included three days of soli-
tary fasting under a makeshift shelter. When Dennis
returned to civilization, he savored a slice of buttered
bread as a feast. He marveled at buses and cars as "shel-
ters" that (a) he did not have to build; (b) had not just a
roof, but sides; (c) had not just sides but adjustable open-
ings in the sides; and (d) moved themselves without
requiring his leg power.

Dennis experienced the truth of Paul's claim: "But if
we have food and clothing, we will be content with that"
(1 Tim. 6:8). As a general perspective on moving out of the
sandwich years nearer to the end of life, we adopt the insight that Paul expressed just before that "we brought nothing into the world, and we can take nothing out of it."

16

The Tie That Binds

Dennis

Some years ago Ruth and I spent a lovely October weekend in Door County, Wisconsin, where we joined several other couples from our Homebuilders Sunday school class at Wheaton Bible Church. As we drove along, the two of us passed the time by singing, as we often do in the car. We particularly enjoyed singing some of the rich hymns of the Christian faith that had shaped our lives over the years. We finally came to "Living for Jesus" and its powerful chorus:

> O Jesus, Lord and Savior,
> I give myself to thee,
> For thou in thy atonement,
> Didst give thyself for me.
> I own no other master.
> My heart shall be thy throne.
> My life I give, henceforth to live,
> O Christ, for thee alone.

Having sung those words with me, Ruth explained how much they had meant to her as a ten-year-old camper. That year her summer church camp had featured that hymn as its theme. In the closing night of a memorable week, she had solemnly sung it with the group around a campfire. Ruth recalled how, in that time of dedication, she had closed her eyes and with her brow furrowed in concentration truly sang those words with all her heart.

Years later, in the car on the way to Door County, she told me, "I *really* meant it, too, and still do when I sing those words." I thought to myself, "Wow, that's powerful! That is the permanent glue that binds my heart to the heart of this remarkable woman."

We had a wonderful weekend with our friends. Then, on Sunday morning, we all gathered around a potbelly stove in the parlor of the inn where we were staying and had an informal worship service. One woman in the group went to a piano and played the music for hymns that people called out spontaneously from the group.

At one point someone asked for the hymn "Living for Jesus." My heart jumped as I remembered the earnest conversation Ruth and I had had in the car two days earlier. Since I knew how much that chorus meant to Ruth, I planned to make eye contact with her when we came to singing that chorus. Ruth was sitting partway around the circle from my seat. I planned to glance up at her, meet her eyes, probably wink, and knit our hearts still closer together in that intimate moment.

The group sang through the first verse and came to the chorus. I glanced up to make my romantic eye contact with Ruth, but—to my surprise—Ruth's eyes were not available. Like the ten-year-old camper, her eyes were closed and her brow was furrowed. She sang those words of dedication once again with all her heart, giving herself still further to the Lord of us both.

I felt a brief twinge of loneliness because I felt left out of Ruth's attention and affection. Then it dawned on me that my sense of security in our marriage rested not on Ruth's love for *me*, but on her dedication to the Lord of all. It was then that I experienced the real meaning of that profound counsel that the apostle Paul gives in starting his instructions to husbands and wives: "Submit to one another out of reverence for Christ" (Eph. 5:21).

When Ruth and I discussed this insight later, we realized that our devotion to each other does not depend on the attractiveness or decency or lovability of our partner. It rests on our surrender to our Lord. Because we have accepted the love of Christ for us both, we respond by continuing to find reasons to love each other.

Our surrender to Christ supplies the proper motivation for all the rest of our behavior, as it can for you. Whether acting as parents to your children, parents to your parents, partner to your spouse, or salt of the earth to your peers, "Whatever you do, work at it with all your heart, as working for the Lord, not for men. . . . It is the Lord Christ you are serving" (Col. 3:23–24).